HANDMADE
TILE

Inspiring | Educating | Creating | Entertaining

Brimming with creative inspiration, how-to projects, and useful information to enrich your everyday life, Quarto Knows is a favorite destination for those pursuing their interests and passions. Visit our site and dig deeper with our books into your area of interest: Quarto Creates, Quarto Cooks, Quarto Homes, Quarto Lives, Quarto Drives, Quarto Explores, Quarto Gifts, or Quarto Kids.

10 9 8 7 6 5 4 3 2 1

ISBN: 978-0-7603-6430-7

Digital edition published in 2019
eISBN: 978-0-7603-6431-4

Library of Congress Cataloging-in-Publication Data is available.

Design: Laura McFadden Design, Inc.
Cover image: Colleen Eversman
Photography: Colleen Eversman except as indicated and:
        Shutterstock: pages 13, 14, 15, 16, 17, 19, 21, 26, 27, 28, 96, 98, 100, 101, 113, 123, 134
            (images 2, 3, and 4), 137, 152, 153, 154, 157, and 159.
        Beth Schaible: pages 49, 50, 51, 52, 53, 55, 56, 57, 58, 59, 60, 61, 62, 103, 104, 105, 106, and 107.
Illustrations: Beth Schaible

Printed in China

FSC
www.fsc.org

MIX
Paper from
responsible sources
FSC® C016973

HANDMADE
TILE

DESIGN, CREATE, AND INSTALL CUSTOM TILES

Forrest Lesch-Middelton

Foreword

Let's begin by acknowledging that tile production can be a maddening affair. Consider the difficulty of making a flat piece of clay stay level and true through the drying and firing process. Then imagine repeating the task thousands upon thousands of times in an effort not unlike that of Sisyphus, the doomed king of Greek mythology.

Such was my viewpoint on tile for the first fifteen years that I worked in clay. I had tried to produce tile, but I did so without finding a resource like this one to guide me. Frustration with my lack of technical understanding clouded my ability to acknowledge the potential of ceramic tile as a medium and, further, to see its relevance to my own artistic practice. I was entirely disinterested in the process as a result.

That changed upon seeing two bodies of work by Cary Esser at Sherry Leedy Contemporary Art in 2016. Not only had the artist disregarded the concerns about process that had stifled me, she used them to great success. In her *Parfleche* series, Cary allowed tile to bend and collapse with such grace, restraint, and fluidity as to reveal the poetics of architecture. In "veils," shown alongside the former, she used flat tile as a canvas for a deeply moving expression of the virtues of glaze. Cary's work proved so transcendent that

it radically altered my perceptions of tile. With newfound interest, I tried again.

It is essential that we as artists disassociate *how* something is made from *what* it is and *why* it is significant. To study tile is to study language, a language used in the histories of architecture, religion, politics, beauty, and so much more. To make tile in your studio is to engage in a global conversation that spans the entirety of constructed things, both in art and in industry. Don't feel hindered—as I did for over a decade—by the technical hardships inherent in trying something new. Instead, feel enlivened by the challenge of problem solving and the opportunity to be part of the conversation.

One of my life's great privileges is my friendship with Forrest Lesch-Middelton. Because our studios are (only) 2,700 miles (4,345 km) apart, our relationship is confined to frequent phone conversations. These treasured discussions often indulge our common interests in music and parenting but just as frequently center on ceramics, politics, and ideas of communication through our work.

Through our friendship I've come to understand how Forrest works, and more importantly, why he works. Forrest has a remarkable appreciation for the history of Islamic tile as an expression of culture. He draws upon this knowledge daily for reasons as simple as the celebration of aesthetics and as complex as developing collective understanding of who we are individually and globally. Forrest has the determination to build a new sense of community from that understanding.

Forrest's studio practice and the quality, consistency, and volume with which he produces tile greatly impress me. The ambitious projects that he has completed and the late nights he *still* endures for the National Council on Education for the Ceramic Arts (NCECA) exhibitions and commissions motivate me, as they should us all. A true renaissance man, Forrest is as exceptional a harmonica player as he is a potter, and as passionate a social activist as he is a designer. His days are packed to the brim with exciting, challenging, and otherwise inspiring creative activities—not the least of which is this book!

Peter Pincus, ceramic artist, assistant professor of art at the College of Art and Design at Rochester Institute of Technology

Contents

Introduction

I often hear stories of how clay changed the lives of my friends and colleagues. For me, it's no different. I would be a completely different person had I not encountered clay: It captivated my mind, occupied my hands, populated my senses, and set me on a path that defined who I am. Along that path there have been many twists and turns, but none so transformative as tile. I started my career as a potter, making vessels. I first "discovered" tile when I started making single tile designs as one-offs for craft shows. Little did I realize, tile would quickly come to stand shoulder to shoulder with vessels. As my career pivoted to making tile, I found it challenged my notions of surface, scale, economy, and design in ways I could not have previously imagined.

In this book, I'll outline much of what I wish I had known when I stumbled headlong into the world of tile with only an academic knowledge of the craft. Admittedly, this book cannot do it all. It is not meant to be the bible on making tile. Tile has a rich history and it would take another book (actually, multiple books!) to cover it all. In the pages that follow, what you'll find is a useful primer. It's a survey of techniques, ideas, and tips that will help you move confidently from inspiration to realization. Through these chapters, you will develop an idea, put it into

context, assess the viability of your project, and install the tile in a lasting and thoughtful way. It will be your guide in problem solving and act as a doorway into further exploration.

The first chapter starts with the basics, taking a quick look at the history of tile as well as the difference between tile made by industry and by hand. Moving on, we'll go through the basics of clay and considerations to keep in mind when making tile. A variety of tutorials will help you create your first tiles, whether you'd like to use a slab roller, an extruder, or roll them by hand. The next chapter will look at the surface of tile, including techniques for glazing, image

transfer, and cuerda seca. It will also cover firing considerations. Before getting into installation, we'll take a detour to examine how tile fits in the context of a space. Finally, we will work our way through installation, including setting, grouting, and sealing.

Throughout the book, you'll find artist features showcasing some of the innovative people making tile today. No matter where you start, or what project you're looking to create, I hope that the information on these pages helps you on your way. Keep an open mind, find inspiration, and enjoy all the possibilities offered by tile.

CHAPTER 1

The Basics

It's true that, in its most basic definition, ceramic tile is a slab of clay cut into a shape and used as a means of decorating and protecting a surface. However, tile can also be a window through which we can glimpse our own history.

I admit that when I first started making tile, I didn't have a clear understanding of which lens to view it through. Although I encountered tile on a daily basis, it was rarely something I noticed. I soon found that if you pay attention, you will see that tile can tell a story. First you must understand the language of tile to understand what it has to share.

In this chapter, we'll take a brief look at tile's history, we'll learn key terminology that will be important throughout the book, and we'll also examine a few key types of tile as well as a handful of common setting styles. Though it's impossible to provide a complete crash course in the history of tile, my hope is that this chapter will begin to change your perspective, so you, too, will fall in love with this unique medium.

Paramont Theater, Oakland, CA, USA

Tile Throughout History

Fired clay is one of the oldest and most enduring manufactured materials on earth; it bares record of the time and place that it was created. In many parts of the world, tile is the most lasting documentation of the people and places in which it is found. The cultural shifts, the commercial and social influences, and the hands in which it was created (and used) are forever ingrained upon its surface. Tile is unique even within the history of ceramics, as its durability and commodification ensure its lasting mark upon and from the history of humanity. Tile alone is the single greatest user of the world's clay resources, and because of this it is both revered and overlooked as a design material.

Topkapi Palace, Istanbul, Turkey

TILE BEFORE THE EARLY TWENTIETH CENTURY

Because of the durability and the relative ease in which ceramic tile is produced, it was used like a skin to cover and protect the sacred buildings of the world's oldest civilizations. As religions evolved, and texts faded and were rewritten, tile is often the most lasting record of the people who came before. Some of the oldest examples of tile are glazed brick from the Pre-Iranian, Elamite civilization circa the third millennium BCE. These brick tiles were used to construct ziggurats and record the legacies of the rulers who had constructed them.

OPPOSITE PAGE TOP: Tile detail from the palace and fortress complex of Alhambra, Granada, Spain.
MIDDLE: Tile detail from Iznik, Turkey; BOTTOM: Detail of decaying tile, Lisbon;
ABOVE: Exquisite example of mosaic work, Hagia Sophia, Istanbul

This incredible example of ancient glazed brick is inscribed with the words of the king who used them to construct the ziggurat which they form. It is seen as both a religious and architectural monument from the time in which it was built.

As more enduring and lasting ceramic wares developed, so did the glazed brick and ceramic tile that was used as an architectural and aesthetic material surpassing the strength and beauty of common earthen brick. One of the most famous examples of ancient ceramic brick tile is the Ishtar Gate commissioned by King Nebuchadnezzar II. Constructed in approximately 575 BCE, the immense Ishtar Gate was the eighth gate of the inner city of Babylon. It was skinned in glazed brick meant to mimic the coveted lapis lazuli, with bas-relief animals and flowers glazed with golden earth tones representing Babylonian gods and goddesses. The Ishtar Gate, being part of the Walls of Babylon, was one of the original Seven Wonders of the World. As its cedar beams and earthen walls crumbled, the ceramic endured. In the photo opposite, you can see how it was recon-structed in the twentieth century. It is now housed in Berlin's Pergamon Museum.

As ceramic technology developed, we began seeing the inconceivably beautiful glazed brick and mosaic tile work that became synonymous with Islamic architecture beginning around the twelfth century. There is no substitute for the scrolling Kufic calligraphy and mind-bending geometric patterns on tile that arose from this period, adorning the great mosques and palaces of the time. We owe a great debt of gratitude to the dedication and elevation of ceramic tile of the Islamic world, as it heralded a global fascination with tile that spread across Northern Africa and into Europe through the Iberian Peninsula, and even into East Asia through both land and sea. As Moorish influence brought techniques such as zellige and cuerda seca across the region, they defined an aesthetic that is still a part of daily life in areas of Spain, Italy, and beyond.

From here began the golden age of tile, starting with porcelain and underglaze influences from Chinese trade along the Silk Road. Iznik, a city in Northern Turkey, went from a thriving earthen-ware pottery center to one of the most influential regions in the history of ceramics. The world experienced the unimaginable crossroads of East and West as the European thirst for Chinese porcelain paired with the Islamic aesthetic and development of underglazed fritware and tile. The deft hand of the Iznik painters combined the best of Chinese floral motifs with unique interpretations of Persian girih tessellations and mosaic to create electrifyingly vivid tile that adorns the palaces and mosques throughout the region to this day.

Forging its place at the top in the vast lexicon of architectural adornments, ceramic tile has become commonplace in virtually every part of the world. Each region now has its own tile history: from the maiolica in-glaze that defines the tile traditions of Spain and Italy, to faience tile in France, and of course Delft tile of the Netherlands with its omnipresent Dutch country scenes directly reminiscent of Chinese blue and white wares. Then there is the tile of the Americas, including the Mexican tile so popular in Southwestern architecture as well as the tile powerhouses that arose during the industrial revolution, including the American Encaustic Tiling Company of Zanesville, Ohio (once the largest tile company in the world) and the Moravian Pottery and Tile Works of Doylestown, Pennsylvania (founded by one of my personal tile heroes, Henry Chapmen Mercer).

Detail of the Ishtar Gate

CONTEMPORARY HANDMADE TILE

Now that you have some understanding of the rich history of tile, imagine adding the technological and scientific advancements of the last one hundred years to the picture. Ceramic engineering, as well as affordable and accessible fossil fuels, technological advancements in kilns, more robust mining practices, and the ability to source information from across the world at the push of a button have all played a key role in the growth of the tile industry. There are very few limitations,

and yet somehow at times it seems like the world of commercial tile has become somewhat stiff. Mass production, though tremendously beneficial for the development of cheaper and more durable tile, often sacrifices aesthetic. It often takes for granted the true potential of the medium.

Although there is no substitute for the unique qualities and tactile nature of handmade tile, many makers today employ modern practices to achieve higher output levels in order to remain competitive in a field dominated by industry. These practices, coupled with a constant eye on aesthetics, and awareness of history and historic practices, can create the perfect marriage of artist and producer.

Like vessel makers, those who make tile by hand can fall into a few categories. I categorize them

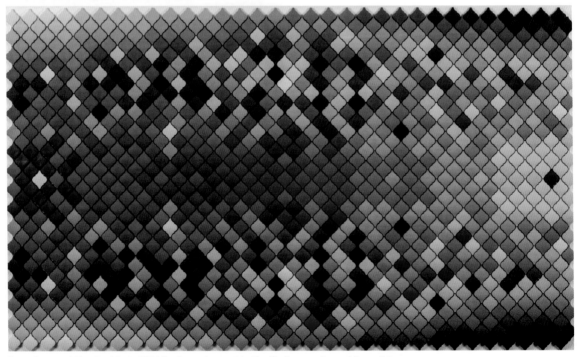

Peter Pincus, *A Familiar Kind of Riddle*, slip-cast porcelain tile. Photos courtesy of the artist.

Collete Crutcher and Aileen Barr, *Moraga Steps*, San Francisco, CA, USA

as "architectural tile makers," "tile muralists," and a third category I call "tile artists." These three categories can overlap and do share some similarities—and many who make tile do all three—but for the sake of conversation I find it easiest to speak about them this way.

- Someone who makes modular tile designed to be used functionally makes architectural tile. This type of tile is meant to be used to protect as well as beautify a space. Architectural tile makers often sell tile by the square foot rather than by the installation. Although primarily made by hand, these tile makers can also employ the use of machinery. Those who make architectural tile usually have a method for making tile en masse, producing hundreds, even thousands, of tiles that are similar in appearance and made for covering and protecting specific areas. (I could be considered someone who makes architectural tile.)

- Tile muralists primarily make permanent, project-based work that is different from location to location and has a certain theme. The work is like a permanent painting made with tile. A muralist would not fulfill an order by the individual piece or by the square foot, but by the whole project. Mosaic artists are muralists. Muralists often work within the public art spectrum.

- Tile artists are not always bound to the medium. They use tile as a means to an end within a single piece of artwork that could illustrate something completely outside the realm of tile itself. Here the object stands alone and can often be impermanent or unaffixed, like a piece of sculpture or a painting. A tile artist has free reign with the medium, with the only thing holding them to the category of tile at all being the tile itself. Jim Melchert, Robert Sperry, Kala Stein, Jason Green, and Jim Bachor are just a few examples of tile artists.

Understanding Tile

Ceramic tile encompasses a broad spectrum, from a covering in a subway that's designed to keep it sanitary to a one-off handmade accent tile or coaster. As a potter, I developed the mindset that industry is competition. However, over time I've grown comfortable with the idea that hand-made and industrially made pots and tile can coexist synergistically. For example, in 1974 Kohler developed an artist-in-residence program where artist participants integrate with Kohler staff and technology and are encouraged to develop new ways of thinking and making. Similarly, the European Ceramic Workcentre in the Netherlands invites artists, designers, architects, and techni-cians to work side by side, share ideas, and grow new understandings of the medium.

In the field, many designers I work with will often use industrial tile to maintain affordability and con-sistency for their clients throughout a project, and then use handmade tile to bring a more personal feel, adding character and context to a job. As a tile maker, I welcome this crossover as it allows me to see my tile in a greater context and understand its use better. Let's explore this intersection.

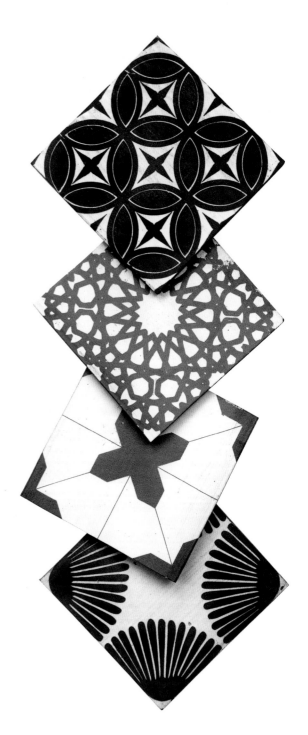

Industrial tile production

INDUSTRY VS. HANDMADE

There used to be a time when a machine-made object, or even a machine itself, was thought of as a novelty. We fantasized about a romantic future when Jetsons-style automatons would serve us dinner, and we would communicate by simply speaking into a picture box. Now we depend on machinery for virtually everything, even building more machinery. All day long we work from behind a desk depending on computers and machines to provide consistent results down to the millionth of an inch, and then we come home exhausted from staring at a box all day. We remind ourselves how important it is to get our hands dirty by toiling in the kitchen, gardening, taking hikes, or even taking a pottery class at the local community studio. We crave narrative. An object's visual history reminds us of our actual history; it makes us feel whole. Our acute appreciation for objects with flaws and eccentricities arises out of a desire for the things we can no longer have enough of: things that are rare and things made by hand. We take in and elevate these handmade objects because they tell us a story rather than provide us with answers.

As this book progresses, you will see references to industry and production methods that are favored by certain tile makers. With tile, the term "hand-made" can have a relatively loose connotation, and you will notice that at times the line between mass-produced and handmade tile may blur to some degree. We will explore a number of ways that you can make tile by hand, and even include equipment to make your life easier while still staying within the realm of the handmade.

I consider handmade tile to be any tile that is either primarily formed or decorated by hand. Many of the tiles in this book are made from methods that purists might consider suspect; artists use machines to form the tile, and yet they may decorate, cut, sand, load and unload it from the kiln, fire it, and pack it by hand. They touch each and every tile, and when you see the final product, there is no question that even with the aid of computers and machines, it is truly handmade.

This book is not meant to be a purist's approach to handmade tile, but one that I hope will encourage you to experiment with different methods that may benefit your level of production—wherever that may lie. From a single backsplash in your own home to owning a small business that depends on machinery to stay competitive, my goal here is to present a broad view of what it can mean to make handmade tile and to give you permission to play and experiment with it.

NOMENCLATURE

There are a few important terms and phrases you should know before launching into making or setting your own tile. Even after a lifetime of working with clay, when I first jumped into making tile I found myself unprepared to speak about my own work within the greater context of the field. This left me at a detriment when speaking with designers and tile setters. For this reason, I want to quickly lay out some words and phrases that might be helpful for you when making, installing, marketing, and speaking about your own tile.

Accent tile: *Tile that is often decorative or different and used as an accent within an installation.*

Base layer or backing: *Any base material over which tile is meant to be installed. Common names are cement board, HardieBacker, and cementitious layer.*

Bullnose tile: *Tile with a finished edge that is meant to be exposed.*

Buttering or back buttering: *Spreading an adhesive coat to the back of a tile prior to setting rather than setting the tile in the adhesive.*

Caulking: *A water-resistant sealing material (usually silicone) designed for filling grout lines when water resistance is paramount, such as in showers.*

Ceramic tile: *This category describes tile that is more durable than terra-cotta tile, yet less than porcelain tile. Ceramic tile is a cousin to porcelain tile, but it has an absorption rate greater than 0.5 percent.*

Cure/cured/curing: *The time in which an adhesive or sealant must be left undisturbed to be considered usable and at full strength.*

Epoxy: *A two-part adhesive that consists of a bonding resin and hardening catalyst. Epoxy is time sensitive, and the two parts must be mixed together to be activated.*

Epoxy grout: *A two-part (or three-part) grout that consists of an epoxy resin and hardening catalyst. Epoxy grout is time sensitive, and the two parts must be mixed together to be activated.*

Field tile: *The primary covering tile in an installation. Often blank tile.*

Float: *There are a few types of floats. A tile float is a rubber rectangular tool (about 3" × 10" [7.5 × 25.5 cm]) with a handle used to push grout into grout lines. A cement float (or bull float) is a long-handled tool with a large flat metal piece on the end used to smooth out concrete after it is poured.*

Floating: *A method of laying tile without attaching it to the subfloor; the tile is literally attached to itself only. This is also the term used for smoothing and finishing a concrete surface.*

Floor tile: *A tile that can withstand floor traffic and has enough traction to minimize slip and fall concerns.*

Spahn & Bontekoe residence in Berkeley, California. House skinned with 4' × 4' (122 × 122 cm) nouovo corso tile manufactured in Italy. Ajay Manthripragada, architect.

Glazed tile: *Tile that has a glazed face. Glaze is used to protect and beautify tile.*

Grout: *A cement-like material used for filling joints between tile. It keeps tile bonded together and makes an entire surface act like one whole object rather than multiple pieces.*

Impervious: *Tile that does not absorb moisture. It is fully vitrified.*

Notched trowel: *A grooved or notched trowel used for applying mortar.*

Pointer: *A small handheld spatula type tool for applying mortar and cement.*

Porcelain tile: *This is the most durable and impervious tile available. It has a water absorption rate of 0.5 percent or less. Porcelain tile is fine grained, fully vitrified, and is usually dry pressed by machine.*

Quarry tile: *Large, machine-made, and unglazed ceramic floor tile that is more than 6" (15 cm).*

Setting tile: *Adhering the tile to a surface with the use of tile mortar or adhesive.*

Spacers: *Rubber inserts designed to evenly space individual tiles from one another to form a consistent grout line when setting tile.*

Substrate: *A subfloor material such as plywood or cement board used as backing beneath or behind tile. It is often used in a different context to describe blank fired tile prior to decorating.*

Terra-cotta tile: *Tile made from earthenware clay (usually red), unvitrified, and not fully impervious to moisture. Terra-cotta is the least durable of the three categories of tile.*

Tile: *For the sake of this book, tile is a modular piece of fired clay used to protect and beautify surfaces such as floors, walls, showers, roofs, and walkways. In a larger construct, tile can also refer to cement, and metal tile, etc.*

Tile adhesive: *Any standard adhesive used for adhering tile to surfaces. Thinset, mastic, and mortar are also common names for tile adhesive. This is sometimes referred to as butter or mud.*

Tile sealer: *A protective liquid applied to finished tile that guards it from exposure and staining, as well as penetration from other materials. It's used to extend the life of the tile.*

Trim: *Various types of tile used for exposed edges and molding.*

Unglazed tile: *Tile that has an unglazed surface.*

Vitrified (vitrification): *Vitrified tile has been fired to a temperature sufficient to form a glassy matrix within the clay that has fully bonded so that it is impervious to penetration by liquids. "Fully vitrified" (often referred to as impervious) tile has an absorption rate of 0.5 percent or less.*

Types of Tile

Most tile is broadly categorized into three different types: terra-cotta tile, ceramic tile, and porcelain tile. As someone who studied ceramics and works with clay as a potter, these descriptions drive me crazy! My understanding of the term "ceramic" is that it is the family that encompasses all types of clay, therefore porcelain, ceramic, and terra-cotta tile should all fall under one heading—ceramic tile. The tile industry separates porcelain, ceramic, and terra-cotta based simply on the levels of vitrification,

Different examples of tile setting styles.

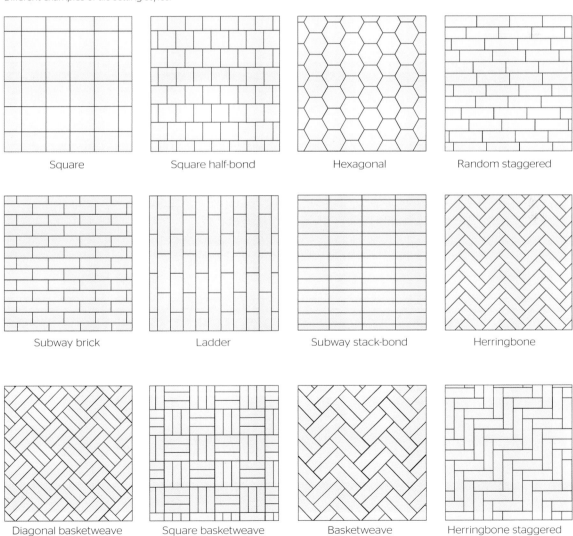

| Square | Square half-bond | Hexagonal | Random staggered |

| Subway brick | Ladder | Subway stack-bond | Herringbone |

| Diagonal basketweave | Square basketweave | Basketweave | Herringbone staggered |

absorption, and durability within the tile itself. Porcelain tile has the highest density and is the least absorbent (0.5 percent or less), followed by ceramic tile, and finally terra-cotta as the softest and most absorbent of all three. The problem here, as you can imagine, is that when someone asks whether you make porcelain tile, they aren't actually asking whether your tile is simply made from porcelain, but if it is completely vitrified. Porcelain is a clay type, and it can be vitrified or not. When someone uses porcelain, it doesn't ensure that it is a durable tile. Yet, in the tile industry, porcelain is a categorization of density rather than a clay type. This misnomer is unique to the tile industry and can cause great confusion because no matter the clay, one tile can be mixed, made, or fired in a way that may make it either more or less absorbent or dense than the other.

Although industry speak is important to understand, as this is a book primarily about handmade tile, I will categorize each tile relative to the clay it is made from; porcelain tile is made of porcelainous clay, stoneware tile is made from stoneware clay, and terra-cotta tile is made from terra-cotta or earthenware.

Aside from the specific clay your tile is made from, you should also be able to determine whether it is going to be used as field tile, accent tile, or ornamental tile. On the following pages, we'll briefly discuss each type.

191st Street Subway, New York City, USA

FIELD TILE

Field tile is the name for any tile that's used to cover most of the square footage within an installation. Field tile does not refer to a production method; rather, field tile simply means it is the dominant tile used for a particular space.

Field tile on a large installation is often industrially made, as it's the cheapest way to provide consistent, sanitary surface covering. Subway tile is a good example. The idea for the subway tile seen in many homes today comes from actual subways. Generally, for this type of tile, aesthetics takes a backseat. The most important attribute is durability and often the ease with which it can be cleaned. Whether it's spilled drinks, or something worse, subway tile needs to stand up to daily wear and tear.

For these reasons, other places you might encounter field tile include restaurants, lobbies, hotel bathrooms, and so on. Though you probably can't make handmade tile for something such as a subway system, with literally tens of thousands of square feet, you can use handmade tile as field tile in other applications. Usually, it's affordability and not durability that keeps some customers from choosing handmade tile.

Aileen Barr, Lincoln Park steps, San Francisco, USA

ACCENT TILE

Accent tile is exactly as it sounds: It enhances or accents an installation dominated by field tile. This type of tile is designed to catch the eye: for this reason, it is often handmade or hand-painted (glazed). These tiles can be a statement piece, such as a cornerstone (which is also architectural tile, see next section).

When it comes to patterned tile, you can see how accent tile may become field tile. The main difference would be whether it is the dominant tile in an installation. I often try to avoid the term when I'm selling tile, because accent tile could become field tile. Calling your own tile "accent tile" may imply that it cannot be used as field tile when that is not the case, and it may cut down on the quantity of tile one might be willing to purchase for their project.

I would also add that trim tile (or tile molding) can be a subsection of accent tile. Just as it sounds, trim is tile used to act as a border to a

TOP LEFT: Tiled stairs, Marrakech, Morocco; **TOP RIGHT:** Delft tile with girl jumping rope, Netherlands; **BOTTOM:** Tin-glazed Delft tiles, Netherlands

tile installation, and it doesn't fit the standard shape or format of the main tile in an installation. Trim tile can include but is not limited to: bullnose, outcorner, incorner, quarter round, half round, cove, cove base, square cap, and more. Though most who make handmade tile don't offer all types of trim, many offer some types to round out their selection.

ARCHITECTURAL TERRA-COTTA

Sometimes referred to as architectural tile, architectural terra-cotta, is generally used on exterior surfaces as a protection against the elements, and to benefit the aesthetic of a building's architecture. As its name implies, it can be quite functional, but the ornamentation that derives from this type of ceramic can also be purely aesthetically driven as well. Different types of brickwork, roof tile, hollow three-dimensional forms, and even gargoyles, downspouts, and other architectural statuary might be considered an architectural form of tile. Architectural terra-cotta is not the focus of this book, but it is important to discuss it briefly and draw attention to how it has inspired tile artists, and how it shares some characteristics with and is also different from the tile discussed in the following chapters.

The earliest types of architectural terra-cotta were found in Chinese, Indian, and Islamic architecture in the form of roof tiles and ornamental brickwork. As materials and styles developed, ornamentation began to blossom, and terra-cotta began replacing the much heavier and more labor-intensive stone pillars and architectural statuary. Much

more convenient than its marble counterparts, hollow architectural terra-cotta could be reproduced with the use of molds, making hollow gutters, downspouts, and ductwork more lightweight, consistent, and economical to produce. Typically hung with metal anchors and backfilled with mortar, this type of work was common as far back as the Roman Empire, and it became ubiquitous with the European architecture of the eighteenth and nineteenth centuries. Much of the American architecture of the nineteenth and early twentieth centuries showcases the beauty of architectural terra-cotta and ornamentation as it blossomed during the Industrial Revolution. Like terra-cotta replacing marble, the advent of synthetic materials that were lighter, cheaper, and more rapidly produced put most terra-cotta companies out of business by the early 1960s.

To this day there are only a handful of companies in the United States that still produce ceramic sewer pipes, roof tiles, and architectural terra-cotta. Although terra-cotta is no longer the best or cheapest choice for skinning a home, some people still choose it for its beauty. Paying homage to the history of tile and architectural terra-cotta, many ceramic sculptors use terra-cotta as a point of departure for its historical significance, and to reference clay's golden age of architectural adornment.

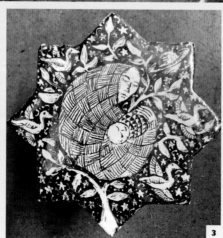

Boris Aldridge

What drew you to making tile?

My father set up a company making English and Delft tiles back in the late 1990s. I joined the company in 2001, and then in 2010 I started my own practice. I wanted to develop the idea of tile as a work of art in its own right rather than just as functional adornment. Working in tile appeals to me for many different reasons, but primarily for my love of clay. It's satisfying to use nothing but your hands, heat, and a bit of glaze to change a lump of dull, brown mud into a glittering, colorful work of art.

Can you briefly walk us through your daily studio practice?

I normally get to my studio around 8:15 a.m. After a sandwich and caffeine, I get straight to work. I spend most of the day applying designs onto glazed tiles using a mixture of brushwork or sgraffito, depending on the tile. This is the most labor-intensive part of making the tile and can take up to four days to complete. If I'm running short of glazed tiles, then I'll make more using clay that I put though a slab roller. I don't do lunch and generally work through until about 4:30 p.m. without a break. If I have enough tiles to fill up the kiln, then I'll load it up and fire it just before I go home. That way, the tiles will be ready for when I come in the next day.

Geometry and history play such a vital role in your work. Can you describe why that is and how these two things inform your daily practice?

For me, the purest and most beautiful application of geometry has always been through tile. From the intricate eightfold patterns of the Alhambra to the majestic tenfold designs of Isfahan, the history of geometry and tile has been inextricably linked. Using the simplest of tools—a compass and a straight edge—it's possible to create extraordinarily complex geometric patterns. I'll often take a break from making tiles to explore new geometric designs and ideas, which I'll then incorporate into my new work.

How do you strike a balance between your pursuits as a maker of both artistic and architectural tile?

Tile lies at the intersection of art and architecture, so for me it's an easy balance to strike. Having said that, I do consider every tile I make to be a work of art. I definitely enjoy making new things rather than reproducing existing designs. I rarely make the same tile twice and, if I do, then they never end up looking the same.

Can you briefly describe your collaborative work with Daniela Yohannes and if or how that has affected you as an artist?

I've known Daniela for a long time and have always had a huge admiration for her work as an artist. Like me, she has work that is influenced and informed by myth, dreams, and storytelling—so our collaboration feels very natural. We've been exploring these themes through a series of tiled pieces ranging from large-scale tiled panels to a single tile. It's been a particularly rewarding and inspiring experience working with an artist of Daniela's standing and talent. We hope to pick up the collaboration again soon.

1 Lustreware star tile; **2** Lustrewarer star and cross panel; **3** Mother and Child; **4** Seven Deadly Sins; Photography courtesy of the artist.

CHAPTER 2

Making Tile

Making tile by hand allows you to be closer to the material and the history of the medium. You have to trust that what you are making by hand—though not always perfectly flat, or an exact color or pattern match—may strike a chord with people who like a good story. Even after taking a tile class, I had no idea how to conceptualize the idea of making hundreds of tiles day in, day out. I thought it would bore me to tears. Years later, a friend reminded me that I am a teacher. That's when I began to approach the medium in the same way I ask my students to approach a new idea: concept first, followed by history, technique, conclusion, and repeat. Now, I am years down the rabbit hole of making tile and I feel I have just scratched the surface!

In this chapter, I outline several methods I recommend for making tile. Even if you are a seasoned tile maker, consider trying each method and be open to new possibilities. Find the time to be a beginner and see where it takes you. Each lesson is based on a proven result, and although some may not click with you, I am confident others will fit your needs. Take good notes, share ideas with friends, and when you aren't making tile or reading this book, dive deep into the history of the tile you love most. When you feel ready, mix things up and see where it takes you.

Clay Considerations for Tile

Before delving into tile making, it is important to discuss your clay choices and to understand clay. Clay choice is everything in ceramics—from durability and firing considerations, to the aesthetics and life of your finished tile. Your clay is the foundation upon which everything is built, so treat it accordingly.

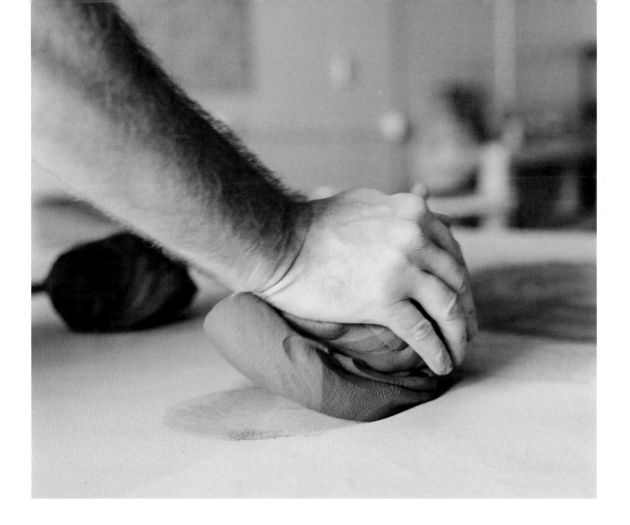

THE BASICS OF CLAY

Virtually any clay can be used to make tile, but some clays work better than others. Historically and geographically, tile making was dependent upon the local materials at hand and the technology available for firing (aesthetics followed thereafter). With advances in mining and globalized trade, we now have an endless variety of material resources and technology at our fingertips. With so many resources available for material and aesthetic inspiration, the biggest hurdle is narrowing down those choices. In terms of clay bodies, the most important technical considerations for any tile maker are warping, durability, and porosity.

Warping is the bane of all tile makers and, to complicate things, it occurs during both drying and firing, for many different reasons. Roughly half of the shrinkage that occurs in clay happens during the drying process, and the warping that occurs at this point is primarily the result of moisture leaving the clay unevenly. There are five relatively simple and surefire ways that can reduce wet-to-dry warping, and I highly recommend that you develop an ingrained awareness of these to aid you in assessing, solving, and avoiding future problems at this stage in the process.

1. Use a clay body high in nonplastic materials or fillers such as grog, molochite, and sand. These materials will cut down on the need for excessive water, which will cut down on warping by allowing your tile to dry more evenly. These fillers create micro channels that allow water to escape evenly throughout the tile.
2. Work as dry as your process will allow. If you are rolling slabs by hand, the clay will have to be wet enough to be pliable, but see how stiff you can handle it before the clay is unworkable. (Less water, less warping.) The same goes for slab rolling, extruding, hand pressing, etc.
3. Move your tile as little as possible throughout the making process. Lifting, flipping, bending, and otherwise disturbing the tile during the making or drying process creates memory within the clay that will come back and haunt you. (Don't even look at it sideways.)
4. When the tiles are dry enough to move without bending, move them to an open-air wire rack. This will help equalize drying with air circulating from above and below.
5. Dry your tile in an area free from breezes, uneven heat, and direct sunlight. New tile makers often forget or omit this consideration, leading to much hand-wringing and head-scratching when trying to assess warping issues.

Durability can refer to both green (unfired) and fired clay. We will focus on fired strength and porosity because green strength is not nearly as important with tile as it is with wheel-thrown or hand built pieces. When considering durability and porosity, become familiar with the term "vitrification." Vitrification is the transformation of any material into glass during the firing process. Clay and glass are the most prominent examples of this. The ring test is a simple (albeit not exactly scientific) way of checking various levels of vitrification. Imagine holding a pot and striking it with your finger. The higher pitched the ringing sound, the glassier and tighter the bond in the material. In other words, it has a higher level of vitrification. Vitrification in clay means it is stronger and less absorbent, therefore in most applications it is less water permeable. Fully vitrified tile is so dense that it may not require glaze to prevent absorption. Tile that is unvitrified absorbs water and can eventually grow bacteria that may break down and cause damage. Unvitrified tiles are far more vulnerable to freeze and thaw damage in cold climates. As water penetrates the tile, it becomes deeply embedded in the clay's matrix. Once freezing occurs, the water expands and breaks the clay apart in a condition called shaling.

Throughout history most tile has been unvitrified earthenware—what the industry lumps into the terra-cotta category. The solution to making unvitrified tile more durable is to glaze and seal it. Glazing earthenware tile goes a long way to prevent moisture penetration because you are adding a glass boundary to the exposed face of the tile. Even with the glaze though, unvitrified tile is still absorbent to a point and certainly can't handle moisture and freezing to the degree that vitrified tile can.

Note: *It's vital to understand and always remember that a kiln load can have varying heat zones, and therefore your tile can be more or less vitrified (porous) throughout a firing. I always err on the side of caution and encourage people to seal my tile as a precaution (and because my tile is not glazed).*

THE FIVE STAGES OF UNFIRED CLAY

There are many stages of workability that can be used to describe unfired clay. I have heard these explained in countless ways. It is important for the purposes of this book that when talking about these stages, we are on the same page, so for the sake of consistency, I will refer to the five stages as follows:

Stage 1: Slip Clay

Slip clay is clay in the wettest form and ranges in consistency from heavy cream to yogurt. If it is pourable, it is slip. Unless used for decorative purposes or the rare slip cast tile, slip clay is the least commonly used in the production of tile. Due to high water content, this stage has the highest rate of shrinkage, which as a result can lead to warping. Slip clays can be made through the addition of water to a clay body, or in many cases, a combination of water and a deflocculant such as sodium silicate or Darvan No. 7. Deflocculating slip allows it to act wet without as much water. This prevents slip clays from oversaturating molds. Deflocculated clays can also be thixotropic, meaning they are thicker or more viscous when standing still, and more fluid when agitated. This, too, can aid in the casting process as they act thicker than other slips. One benefit to using slip clay to make tile is that when poured, it retains very little memory. Though this is great, it also must dry for longer, so patience is of utmost importance when making tiles from slip!

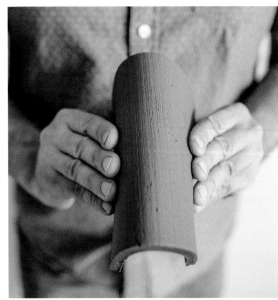

Stage 2: Wet or Bagged Clay

Wet clay refers to clay that is right out of the bag or out of the mixer. Wet clay is probably what you think of when you want clay that's at the most plastic and workable stage. Bagged clay has been mixed from dry clay with water and should have sufficient time to age. The aging allows for full saturation of clay particles, and in many cases encourages beneficial bacterial growth that can help break down the clay and inhibit plasticity. It is perfect for throwing on the wheel, coiling, and making slabs by hand or slab rolling, at this stage, but has less structural integrity. Because of the relatively high moisture content, tile may warp when not handled properly.

Stage 3: Leather-Hard

This stage refers to clay that is similar in feel to a thick leather strap, like a belt. Leather-hard clay has lost enough of its moisture so that it is bendable, but it is no longer pliable like wet clay. It is workable, but no longer wedge-able. At this stage, the clay can handle more weight without squashing or distorting, and it can also be bent without breaking easily. Most tile extruding pug mills, like the one I use, take advantage of clay that is between the wet and leather-hard stage. Hydraulic presses can handle "stiff mud" consistency clay that is a little closer to the leather-hard stage than wet clay stage.

Stage 4: Chocolate-Hard

Chocolate-hard clay is just as it sounds . . . no, not tasty. This clay has a consistency like that of a chocolate bar. Chocolate-hard clay has yet to lose all of its moisture, though it can no longer bend without breaking, and it takes on moisture slower than wet or dry clay. A chocolate-hard piece of clay is at its most durable prior to firing in that it won't distort if you bump it, and it also won't shatter the same way a bone-dry piece will if it is bumped or dropped. Chocolate-hard clay can be carved or shaved without creating dust, and it is at the ideal stage to move from the ware board to the drying rack because of its firmness. Chocolate-hard clay can be put in a kiln on a drying cycle, but it should not be fired up rapidly until bone-dry.

Stage 5: Bone-Dry

Bone-dry is used to describe clay that won't get any drier without the heat of the kiln. Clay at this stage has lost all of its regular moisture and snaps when you try to bend it. This is the best stage for sanding to remove burrs and smooth down edges. Bone-dry clay is fragile, and if bumped, cracked, scratched, or disfigured, it is incredibly difficult to repair. This is because bone-dry clay has already shrunk up to half of its total shrinkage. Any attempt at using slip clay to repair it would create incompatible shrinkage and lead to cracking.

Note: Clay dust can pose an extreme hazard to your lungs. Always wear respiratory protection when creating airborne particulate from clay dust. Any sanding must be done outdoors or in an environment with proper ventilation designed for sanding tile.

SPECIAL CLAY CONSIDERATIONS FOR TILE

In tile making, it is best to work with clay that is as dry and stiff as possible while still being able to control and manipulate it. Moisture equates to shrinkage, and shrinkage is when warping occurs. In the industry, there is a process called dust pressing, where clay powder is compressed with only 8 percent water content. This allows for immediate firing and virtually zero green shrinkage. You can actually pick up a dust-pressed tile the minute it is made and snap it in half—it has no plasticity at all. This is an extreme example of using stiff clay, yet it emphasizes how water content can affect warping.

Your method of making tile will factor into what type of clay you use. Bagged clay is roughly 25 to 30 percent water. It is soft and perfect for rolling slabs by hand because a rolling pin can only apply so much pressure and your body has a limit to what it can do. A softer clay is necessary for this method. As a slab roller is a simple machine, it is able to handle clay that is stiffer than a rolling pin can handle. More complex tile making equipment such as tile extruding pug mills can handle clay that is even stiffer, followed by hydraulic presses with plaster molds that can handle much stiffer clay, and finally hydraulic presses with metal molds are able to manage clay that is too stiff to work by hand.

I make my tile with a mix of commercial bagged clay and powdered dry mix of the same clay body as an additive. A little known fact is that most manufacturers will sell their commercial clays in powdered form. Mixing bagged with powdered clay can be done by hand or in a clay mixer. This creates a consistency between that of bagged clay and leather-hard clay. Another option for removing water content from your clay is to leave bagged clay out in thick coiled arches or small

blocks long enough to achieve your desired firmness. Pitfalls to this method are that it sometimes takes hours, the clay can dry unevenly, and when you go back to check on it, it may be too dry and unworkable.

Note: *I prefer commercial clay to batch clay mixed in my own studio because it saves time and energy, and it allows me to focus on the end product rather than the job of clay management. Letting go of tasks that are not 100 percent critical to my aesthetic, and that the industry will do better, cheaper, and more expediently, saves me time and money.*

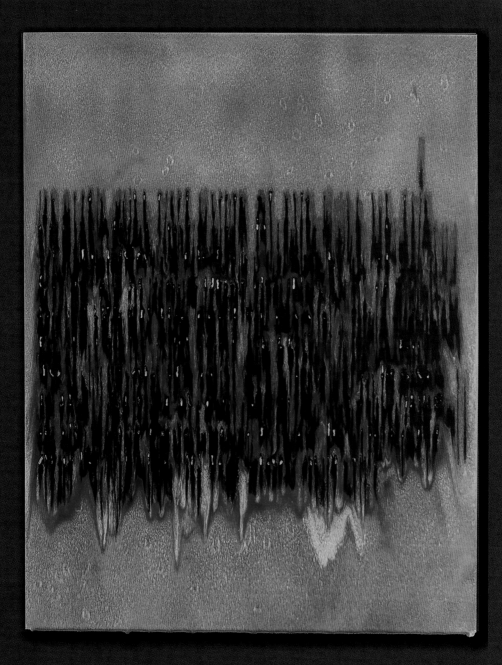

Bobby Silverman

Throughout your career there have been some distinct shifts in your work. How would you describe what it is that you do and the progression that led to where you are today?

There have been three consistent threads throughout my work: color, process, and the phenomenological aspects of the material, which play an important role in what I do. This all began with pots and later with my large-scale and commercial tiles. The idea is to take objects that we take for granted—or assume to be more mundane—and imbue them with a higher level of meaning using concepts unique to ceramics, such as reflection, gravity, translucency, and luminosity.

It all started with a trip to China in 2000 where I saw a whole community in Jingdezhen working with large-scale tiles and using them as paintings. They were taking their traditional pots, flattening them out, and showing them as large paintings on tile. I took on the challenge of illustrating how this can this be done in Western culture.

For example, I've been using the gravity of the fired glaze material to blur text in a way that was its own narrative, of sorts, by taking it one step further into a more abstracted image and meaning. This hints at the history of Islamic tile, where calligraphy becomes partly or totally illegible. It can be abstracted to mean nothing at all, or something quite profound, depending on how you perceive it.

How do you separate the commercial tile from the more conceptual tile you make? Or are they related?

Because scale and color are aspects of my work, architects and designers began to take note. I eventually decided that my commercial tile could be an extension from what I already made. As my handmade tile dealt with light and reflection, my commercial tile does the same but to a different and more literal extent. Though I don't create the commercial work by my own hand, it is certainly informed by the ideas behind my handmade work, allowing for great cross-pollination.

Why, or how, is content important in tile?

The wall can be a political space. Tile and architecture can be something other than decorative; they can have meaning. Whether it's Islamic tile, Chinese wall posters, or Russian architecture, there are ways in which we can use architecture to challenge norms.

What excites you or bothers you about some of the tile you see today?

Any problems I have with tile stem from the internal, self-referential dialogue in the field; it's a conversation within the work that is reflective of the community rather than the time and place we are in. Fortunately, we are now seeing other artists embrace clay in a more contemporary way. I see this as similar to what happened to photography in the '70s: artists got into the medium and they blew up the community (in a good way). I think clay needs more of that.

1 Emerson Beauty (second half), 2014; **2** Hotel Foshan, detail, 2015; **3** Hotel Foshan, lobby, 2015; **4** Proposal for The MTA and Grand Central Station, 2009; Photography courtesy of the artist.

Rolling Slabs for Tile by Hand

Rolling tiles by hand is as simple as it gets and requires the lowest investment of equipment. However, there are significant downsides to this method as well. It is more labor-intensive than others and can be difficult to achieve the consistent results of a slab roller. Long-term, it is also much harder on your body due to the repetitive motions that accompany the use of a rolling pin. It is still probably the best place to begin as it will allow you a low-cost way to start familiarizing yourself with the tile-making process.

At the end of this tutorial, you will have three 15 × 15 × ½" (38 × 38 × 1.3 cm) slabs drying on a piece of drywall (see page 48) and ready for the cutting process described on page 54. It's important that you use clay that is either straight from the bag, or a clay of similar consistency, for this tutorial. Stiff clay will not work well.

Rolling Slabs for Tile with a Slab Roller

Slab rollers are a great tool for making quality tile with a handmade feel, but with increased production compared to rolling by hand. As long as you pay attention throughout the process, you'll find it's much easier to get consistent results with a slab roller than with a rolling pin. Slab rollers reduce stress on the body from repetitive motions and make it possible to outsource—or partner up—when producing tile. If you are looking to get into greater tile production, there may soon come a point where you'll want to train an assistant on the slab roller.

By the end of this tutorial, you'll have a 15" × 15" (38 × 38 cm) and ⅜" (1 cm)-thick slab on drywall that has never been picked up and has been minimally handled. In other words, this tutorial will take you from a bag of clay to the cutting section on page 54. This tutorial is easiest if you use clay straight from the bag. However, it is possible to use raw clay, reclaimed clay, and so on. Just make sure to review the section on page 38 to make sure your clay is ready for the roller.

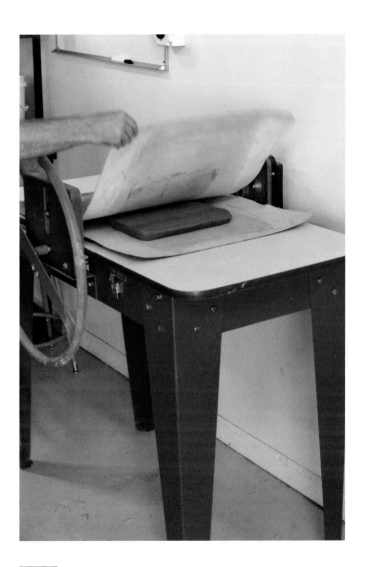

Tools and Materials

- 25 lb (11.3 kg) of bagged clay
- slab roller
- 2 sheets of canvas, approximately 24" × 30" (61 × 76 cm) (I use a printing blanket, see page 53.)
- mallet
- 2 pieces of drywall board (see page 48), approximately 18" × 24" (46 × 61 cm)

Instructions

Remove the clay from the bag and lay it on its side. From a rectangular block, cut the clay into three equal-size sections, about 6" × 2" × 12" (15 × 5 × 30.5 cm). Your block may be slightly different, but you'll want to end up with sections that are flat and wide, and about 2" (5 cm) deep. If your clay comes in cylindrical pugs, you can use the mallet to flatten it into a slab roughly 2" (5 cm) in depth **(1)**.

Once you have your pieces divided out, place a sheet of canvas on the slab roller and then transfer one piece of clay to the canvas. Set the slab roller to 1½" (4 cm). If starting with a thicker slab of clay, set the slab roller to ½" (1.3 cm) lower than the thickness of your clay.

Note: *The thickness of your canvas or printing blanket (see page 53) when subtracted from the measurement on the slab roller will mean that your resulting slab will be less than the 1½" (4 cm) reading on the slab roller's guides. That is intentional.*

With the mallet, pound down the leading edge of the slab. The goal is to taper the end that goes into the slab roller. (Be careful not to pound it thinner than 1½" [4 cm]) **(2)**.

Move the clay so that it is about 1" (2.5 cm) away from the rollers on the canvas. Cover the clay with the second sheet of canvas so that the clay is sandwiched between two sheets **(3)**.

1

2

Begin rolling by pushing the clay with one hand into the slab roller until the rollers bite. Once the slab roller has engaged, flip the top canvas over the rollers so you can see what is happening as the clay is being fed through the slab roller. Crank the slab roller and continue rolling until the clay fully exits the other end **(4)**.

Push the slab back through the roller in the opposite direction. This doesn't compress the clay much more, but it will allow you to roll the second pass on the same side without picking up the clay.

Peel the top sheet of canvas off the slab and place it back over the top of the rollers to get it out of the way. (You can leave the edge between the rollers.) Rotate the slab 90 degrees. If possible, slide the clay to move it rather than picking it up, but you may have to pick it up if the clay is stuck to the canvas **(5)**.

Set the rollers down ½" (1.3 cm) (or to 1" [2.5 cm] if your first pass was at 1½" [4 cm]). Most slab rollers can handle the tension of at least ½" (1.3 cm) increments, but if your slab roller is older, less durable, or if you are unfamiliar with the tension on your slab roller, make each of the subsequent passes ¼" (6 mm) at a time until you are more familiar with its limits.

Repeat the process of passing the clay through the roller. For this pass you do not need to pound down the leading edge. Pay attention to the tension of your roller. If the clay does not go through easily, back off about ⅛" (3 mm) and proceed down to a 1" (2.5 cm) slab in multiple passes.

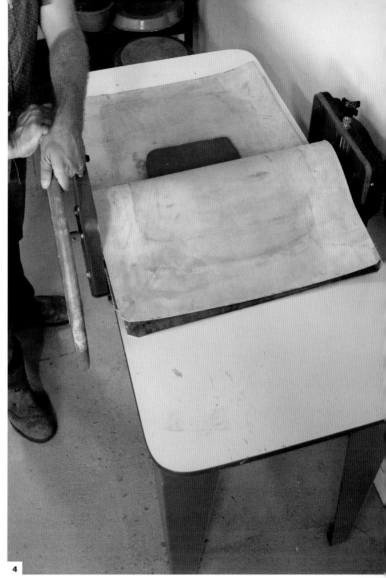

4

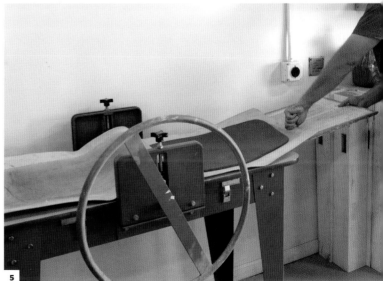

5

Repeat the process of backing the slab through the roller and rotating it 90 degrees each time to prevent uniform particle alignment. This time you will probably need to pick up the clay to rotate it as the slab is getting bigger and harder to slide. Set the slab roller down another ½" (1.3 cm), so it's at about ½" (1.3 cm) depth, and repeat the process of passing the slab through the slab roller.

The finished slab is about 15" × 15" × ⅜" (38 × 38 × 1 cm) and you get three of these per 25 lb (11.3 kg) block of clay, though it may vary depending on your starting dimensions.

Carefully move this slab from the roller to your work surface. I recommend sliding the canvas with the slab on top directly from the roller to a board to prevent bending, and then using the board to carry the slab to your work surface.

Lay a second piece of drywall directly on top of the slab. Place one hand on top, one hand on bottom, and flip the slab so that it's now resting directly on the piece of drywall. Set the slab sandwich on the table. Remove the sheet of drywall that's now on top and then carefully peel the canvas off the slab, starting at one corner **(6-8)**.

6

Note: *For tile, it's very important that this final measurement is consistent. If ½" (1.3 cm) is your final depth, you'll want to make sure that the slab roller is set to exactly ½" (1.3 cm) and that you're using the same canvas for all your tile. If you need to fine-tune your measurement and run the slab through the roller an extra time, that's okay.*

Note: *If you have to transfer the slab of clay without a board, pick it up using the canvas as a support. Never put your hands directly on the clay, or even through the canvas, if you can avoid it. You'll have the best support carrying the canvas by its narrower sides. Pull the canvas tight enough to avoid bending and distorting the slab.*

The Printing Blanket

When I was teaching at a junior college, I stumbled upon a unique tool that offset printers use called a printing blanket. It's essentially a piece of rubber that's about 24" (61 cm) wide by 30" long (76 cm) that is laminated on one side with a soft piece of canvas.

I've found it to be perfect for rolling slabs became the rollers really bite the rubber on one side and the canvas side is perfect for clay. While they're flexible, they're stiffer than a thick piece of canvas. This means when you pick it up off the slab roller, you have more support and your

slab won't bend in half. It's yet one more way to prevent warping—which is the key to making tile! They also make a great makeshift wedging surface when in need.

Some ceramic suppliers have started carrying printing blankets. Call your local supplier or one of the major suppliers found on page 200. You may also get lucky if you call local offset printers. Many will discard printing blankets near the end of their lives for free—and they still work perfectly fine in the ceramic studio. Just as you would with canvas, you'll want to keep separate sets of printing blankets on hand for different clay bodies.

Cutting Clay into Tiles

Just like forming clay into slabs or sheets, cutting clay into tiles can be done in numerous ways. In this section, I cover a few ways to cut squares: by hand, with a tile cutter, and with a block. When cutting tile, it's important to keep shrinkage in mind. My clay shrinks 10 percent, so if I want a 4" × 4" (10 × 10 cm) finished tile, I need to start with a 4.4" × 4.4" (11.2 × 11.2 cm) square template or tile cutter to account for shrinkage.

This tutorial picks up where the slab rolling tutorials end. In other words, it assumes you have a ⅜" (1 cm) slab on a sheet of drywall, ready to work. Once we clean up the slab and transfer it to the work surface in this tutorial, you will need to let it dry overnight before cutting the tiles.

Tools and Materials

For all methods

- pre-rolled slab on a piece of drywall (see page 48)
- fettling knife (I recommend Dolan.)
- sponge
- red polymer rib, such as by Mudtools
- metal square
- triangle
- wire rack

For cutting by hand

- ruler with a raised spine
- carpenter's square
- pencil
- needle tool (optional)
- pizza cutter

For cutting with a tile cutter

- tile cutter (with a plunger or a block to assist in even tile removal)
- carpenter's square
- pencil
- needle tool (optional)
- cornstarch

For cutting with a block form

- a piece of wood with a handle, cut into a 4.4" × 4.4" (11.2 × 11.2 cm) square (or the size of choice for your tile)

Instructions

No matter which method of cutting you decide to use, you will first need to clean the slab. Start by running the rib gently over the surface of the slab, and then cut about ½" (1.3 cm) off the edge of the slab all the way around to prevent micro cracks, formed on the edges during the rolling, from propagating. Place the blade about ½" (1.3 cm) from the edge and use your middle finger as a guide on the outside edge of the slab **(1)**.

Once the slab has had ample time to dry to a leather-hard consistency, transfer it from the drywall to your work surface. Letting it stiffen up to this point before moving is key to preventing distortion and warping when removing the slab from the drywall. (Drywall is not a particularly durable surface for cutting as it is easily damaged.) Ideally, you'll want to work on a canvas-covered table. It is best to transfer the slab to the corner of the table

1

for ease of working rather than a single edge or middle of the table.

CUTTING TILE BY HAND

Before you begin, make sure your slab is at the soft leather-hard stage.

Using a carpenter's square and a pencil or needle tool, mark the entire slab with light guidelines for cutting. To do this, line up the square across the top and mark from one edge all the way across to maximize the number of tiles you can cut from one slab of clay. Then use the other axis of the carpenter's square to mark a similar perpendicular line. (Starting your lines from the middle could result in losing two edges of precious prepared clay that could otherwise become tile.) Use the carpenter's square to make a series of light lines in 4.4" (11.2 cm) intervals below and parallel to the top line. Then lay out perpendicular lines in the clay in the same manner from left to right (2).

Now that grid is laid out, place the square or a large ruler on the first cut line. Use a pizza cutter to cut the line, starting at the edge closest to you and pushing it away from you. Pay careful attention to keep the pizza cutter perfectly upright. If you struggle with this, try using a ½" (1.3 cm)-thick piece of wood instead of the ruler or square as a brace to keep the pizza cutter vertical (3).

2

3

___

Note: *Why worry about keeping the cutter vertical? If the cut isn't straight up and down, you'll undercut one tile and distort another's top edge, which will be a problem when grouting.*

4

After you've cut all the lines in one direction, move around the table to access the other side of the slab. Cut the remaining lines, again starting at the edge closest to you so you can roll the pizza cutter out and away from you **(4)**.

Once all the lines have been cut, you should separate them as soon as possible. It's better for the tiles to dry with space between them. Fortunately, now that you have smaller pieces, it's safer to handle them without the risk of warping.

Carefully transfer the tiles to a wire rack. If you pick up any tiles that have imperfect edges, you'll need to make a judgment call on whether to discard the tile or attempt to clean up the edges. For minimal adjustments, I'd recommend waiting until the clay is chocolate-hard and using a rough cleaning pad or damp sponge to finesse the problematic edges **(5-6)**.

CUTTING TILE WITH A TILE CUTTER

Before you begin, make sure your slab is at the medium stiff stage of leather hard.

Just like when cutting by hand, you'll want to maximize the number of tiles you can get from a slab. However, with the tile cutter you don't need to grid out the whole slab. Use a carpenter's square and a pencil or a needle tool to lightly mark a line across the top edge of the slab.

Make sure the tile cutter is clean, especially on the interior edge. Powder the edges of the cutter lightly with cornstarch to aid the tile in releasing from the cutter. Press the tile cutter into the clay **(7)**.

If your tile cutter has a plunger, you'll be able to use that to release the tile. If your tile cutter does not have a plunger, I recommend cutting a piece

---

Note: *Tile cutters require a good amount of force to make perfect cuts. Using a durable cast cutter allows me to work the tile at a stiffer stage to prevent warping. Working on the floor, and at times stepping on the tile cutter, can be a way to achieve the proper force.*

5

7

6

8

of wood that's about ⅟₁₆" (2 mm) smaller than the interior dimension of the tile cutter. If you're unable to do this, a bit of extra cornstarch can help the tile cutter release the tile.

Once the tile is released, continue with the tile cutter, working across one row and then moving down across the slab. I recommend cutting each tile about ⅛" (3 mm) from the previous one to avoid any compression and distortion from the previous cut **(8)**.

When all the tiles have been cut, check their edges for burrs. Most minor burrs should come right off by rubbing them with your thumb. Unlike when cutting by hand, you should not have any problem with undercuts when using a tile cutter. After checking for burrs, you can move all the tiles to the wire rack to dry.

CUTTING TILE WITH A BLOCK FORM

Before you begin, make sure your slab is at the soft leather-hard stage, or even closer to the wet stage.

Cutting with a block is exactly what it sounds like—using a block as a tile mold. It is a proven method that is very simple and effective, but I have seldom seen the method used in the West.

To try this technique, you will need a wood block cut to the size and shape you want for your tile, with some sort of handle on the back. The actual technique is a hybrid of the two previous techniques. Trace a line at the top of the slab when using the tile cutter to make sure you're making efficient use of your slab.

Set the block against the top edge of the line at the left (or right) side of the slab. Using a fettling knife or pizza cutter, cut out the tile all the way around the block. It is that simple! For this method, you can either move on to the second tile, leaving ⅛" (3 mm) in between tiles, or you can remove the first tile. The advantage of removing the first tile before proceeding is that you won't accidentally cut into the tile or otherwise damage it while you continue to work. Although this method may sound awkward and oversimplified, when practiced it can be used extremely quickly and effectively, and it reduces the need for costly tools **(9)**.

You may need to let the tiles stiffen up a little before you set the finished tiles on the wire rack as you would with the other methods. Check for undercuts or other edge irregularities as you would when cutting tile by hand.

9

CLEAN UP AND DRYING

If you're able to recycle scraps of clay, now is the time to do it. Clay at the stiff leather-hard stage, used in the tile cutter method, may be too far gone for simple reclaiming. However, the other two methods should leave you with clay that's easy to throw back in a bag, rewet, and wedge a day later.

When letting the tiles dry, follow these best practices:

- Once the clay is dry enough to withstand the texture of a wire rack, put it there until it is bone dry. In other words, do not compress the tiles or place them under plastic.

- Nothing should be touching the tiles, including other tiles. Leave a ½" (1.3 cm) space between them.

- Don't handle the tiles any more than you have to (say, for decoration).

- Breezes are a major culprit for warpage when tile is drying, so it is extremely important to let the tiles dry untouched in a room, or corner of a room, with no breeze.

Note: *When cutting around the block you'll want to cut a little past the edge of the block to ensure competent, clean cuts.*

Extruding Tiles

This section is for the tile maker who wants to increase their production level and bring in the equipment needed to make upward of five hundred tiles a day. While true mass production is hard to achieve in your personal studio, extruding is a common way of making tile in larger quantities as it improves consistency and flow, plus it eases wear and tear on your body.

This tutorial will teach you how to mix and extrude your own tile from a pug mill in batches of about 120 lb (54.4 kg) at a time. This is enough clay to create about 120 tiles measuring 6.6" (16.8 cm). If you'd like to make more or less, scale the batch as needed. The extrusion made from a pug mill or wall-mounted hand extruder is akin to a slab that is made on a slab roller, but quicker, more evenly formed, and densely compressed. You can cut and decorate the slab in the same manner you would any other slab made for tile.

Tools and Materials

- pug mill
- expansion chamber for the pug mill
- end cap die for the expansion chamber with a ⅜" (1 cm)-tall × 6.6" (16.8 cm)-wide opening
- 100 lb (45.4 kg) of bagged clay
- 20 lb (9 kg) of powdered dry mix of the same clay body (see page 41)
- baker's speed rack (These racks hold 20 drywall boards and are fitted with casters, which lets me move one hundred and twenty 6" [15.2 cm] tiles around the studio at once.)
- 20 drywall boards cut to 18" × 24" (45.5 × 61 cm) (for transferring and drying the tile)
- fettling knife
- pizza cutter or rotary cutter
- opaque deflocculated slip (½ gallon [2 L], enough for dipping a brush into)
- 6" (15.2 cm) hake brush
- wire rack

Instructions

Before you begin, make sure your pug mill is fitted with the expansion chamber and the desired die for the size of tile you will be making. This tutorial is for 6.6" × 6.6" × ⅜" (16.8 × 16.8 × 1 cm) tiles.

Check that the consistency of your clay is stiffer than clay you would roll by hand or through the slab roller but still flexible. The pug mill extrudes tile with such pressure that wet clay can tear apart as it is leaving the machine. Stiffer clay resolves this problem and reduces future warping by reducing water content. To stiffen up the clay, you can either mix in powdered clay, leave blocks of clay to dry out a little ahead of time, or add powdered dry mix to the pug mill in intervals. The latter method is what I recommend and teach here.

Cut a block of clay into thirds, adding one-third of a block and then one generous scoop of dry mix to the pug mill. Do this until the chamber seems full. Close the lid and run the mill on "mix" for two to three seconds to clear space for the next round of loading. When full, the mixing chamber of my pug mill can hold about 120 lb (54.4 kg) of clay. (The amount in yours may be different.)

Run the pug mill on mix for about 3 to 4 minutes and then turn on the vacuum and de-air the clay to between 25 to 30 lb of vacuum while on the mix cycle.

Make sure your receiving table is at a height so that the top of the drywall board is in line with the bottom of the opening of the extruder die. Flip the operation switch from "mix" to "pug" and press the run button. You should soon see a ribbon of beautiful de-aired tile coming from the end of the pug mill **(1)**.

As the clay is extruded from the pug mill onto the drywall board, it may begin to slightly track left or right. It is important that the clay not track or the final tile will not be straight. To prevent tracking, keep your hand near the end of the ribbon, ready to apply the slightest pressure to the front of the ribbon on one side or the other to keep the clay in a straight line.

Stop the pug mill when the clay ribbon nears the end of the board. Cut the ribbon free on the end closest to the pug mill with your fettling knife and push the drywall board forward to open up a space for the next ribbon.

Extrude a second ribbon in the same manner as before, parallel to and about ½" (1.3 cm) from the previous ribbon. Once completed, you should have two parallel ribbons of the same length on the drywall board. Place the board on the rack and add a new board to the front of the pug mill to catch the next ribbon. Repeat the same process until the rack is completely full. In my case, this is twenty boards and forty ribbons of clay (2).

After extruding, drying the tile correctly is crucial. The first drying occurs just after the tile is extruded onto the drywall board. After it is extruded, the tile ribbon should be allowed to sit for up to an hour or so before cutting with a felting knife or pizza cutter. The drywall pulls moisture from the clay, which will allow you to transfer an image, paint, add surface design, and cut the tile without easily bending or compressing it.

2

Note: *Even though I explain using a pug mill—which is what I use—to make tile in the main tutorial, you can also use a hand-operated clay extruder with an expansion box on the end. Though a hand operated extruder may create some bending and warping issues, it is still a decent option for handmade tile when used correctly. Below is an example of making trim tile with a hand-cut die on a hand-operated extruder.*

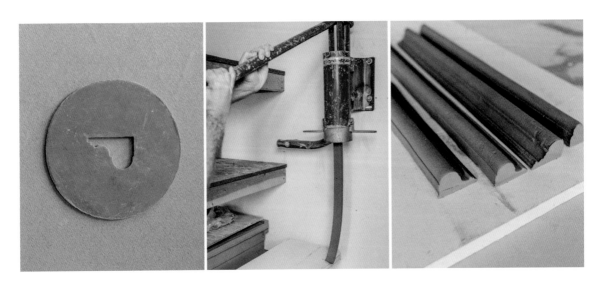

Making a Tile Mold

Pressing tile is a time-tested technique that offers artists the option to mass produce the exact same tile with relief in the form of carved or raised elements, texture, or embossed and debossed surfaces. This method is unique from the others outlined in this chapter in that it uses a one-piece mold made by hand which can be used repeatedly, yielding the same result.

To cast, we'll use plaster, which has been used as a mold-making tool for millennia. When plaster is mixed with water, a chemical reaction occurs that allows it to be pourable, taking on the negative shape of whatever it comes in contact with, and in a short period of time hardens to a dense and absorbent solid. By the end of this tutorial, you'll have a plaster mold ready to use for making tile using the tutorial on page 71.

Hand-pressed tiles from Blue Slide Art Tile, Point Reyes, California, USA

Tools and Materials

- 1 blank 4" × 4" (10 × 10 cm) leather-hard tile with relief or texture
- 2.8 lb (1.27 kg) of pottery plaster no. 1
- 1 gallon (3.8 L) bucket filled with 2 lb (0.9 kg) of cold tap water
- 5 gallon (19 L) bucket half filled with water (for cleanup)
- set of 4 cottle boards (see page 73)
- four 3" (7.5 cm) c-clamps
- 18" × 18" (45.5 × 45.5 cm) sheet of acrylic glass
- 18" × 18" (45.5 × 45.5 cm) sheet of plywood (can be larger)
- 2 lb (0.9 kg) of scrap clay
- soft paintbrush
- latex or rubber gloves
- mold release agent (Murphy's Oil soap works great!)
- rubber mallet
- surform rasp
- sponge

Making the Tile Blank

The first step in pressing tile by hand is making the tile "master" from which you will create your mold. Start by making a blank tile that is exactly the size of the finished tile you would like to recreate with the mold. In this case, I am working with a 4" × 4" (10 × 10 cm) tile. This tile blank should be allowed to dry to the leather-hard state so that you can add design elements and texture to it. It should have absolutely no undercuts.

From this simple tile blank you could easily make your mold, but without surface texture or ornamentation it would defeat the purpose of a press mold. Instead, you should add sprigging, texture, embossment, or whatever design work you'd like to change the surface of your tile. Here I have simply rolled a textured roulette across the tile's surface to create an embossed effect. You can add relief in the form of a pattern, a piece of lettering, an animal, and so on **(1)**.

Just like with the tile blank itself, make certain that your relief work has no undercuts or it won't release from the tile mold once it is poured and in use. Once you are satisfied with your tile master it is time to make the mold.

1

Note: *To avoid undercuts, set the tile on the table and look at it from the side. All sides of the tile should be just a hair narrower on top. The reason is that if it were the opposite, and the bottom were narrower, you'd have a situation where your tile would be trapped by the mold and would never come out after the plaster has dried.*

Affixing the Tile and Making
a Dam for the Plaster

The first step in making a mold of your tile is affixing it securely to a smooth surface. I recommend acrylic glass or a laminated composite material as they are both smooth and easy to clean up. First, dampen the underside of your tile with a sponge, just enough so that it can just slightly slide around on top of the acrylic glass. Next, with a slight downward pressure, slide the tile back and forth so it becomes a little less slippery and it creates suction. Test the tile by gently pulling upward. If it comes off the acrylic glass, you either used too much or too little water when making the bond and you'll need to try again. Once it is secure, do a visual check around the perimeter of the tile to ensure it has no undercuts between it and the acrylic glass. Finally, roll a tiny coil of clay and blend it between the tile and acrylic glass to ensure a good bond and reduce the possibility of undercuts—the tile should sit clean and flush with the acrylic glass.

Now that the tile is secure, place the cottle boards around the tile, leaving a space of about 2" (5 cm) between the interior edge of the boards and the tile itself **(1)**.

Next, clamp the boards together and use coils of clay about the size of your pencil to seal up all the interior and exterior edges between the cottle boards and the acrylic glass, and in the wall joints between each board. You should now have a tile that is affixed to the acrylic glass, surrounded by the cottle board dam, which is sealed on all edges **(2)**.

Use the soft paintbrush to apply the mold release agent to the tile, the acrylic glass, and the interior walls of the cottle boards. This step must be done with great attention as the mold release agent prevents the plaster from sticking to everything.

Brush the mold release conservatively, but thoroughly. You should see that the tile and walls are damp with the release agent, but no puddles should be present. Let this set for about 10 minutes so that all the tiny bubbles settle out while you mix the plaster.

Mixing and Pouring the Plaster Mold

Pour 2 lb (0.9 kg) of cold water into the clean 1-gallon (3.8 L) bucket. Sift the 2.8 lb (1.27 kg) of plaster into the water evenly, one handful at a time, until it is all used up. It should mound slightly, and the exposed plaster mounds will begin to wick up the water in a short period of time. Allow the mixture to sit undisturbed for 3 to 4 minutes. This crucial step allows the plaster to saturate fully and the chemical reaction to start the hardening process. Next, using a gloved hand, mix the plaster slowly in a side-to-side motion, making sure that you do not stir in air, and ensuring that the slurry is even and becomes the consistency between heavy cream and pancake batter. Use the wooden handle of your rubber mallet to firmly tap the wall of the bucket to drive out any air that may have been trapped **(1)**.

To test whether the plaster is ready to pour, drag your finger through the liquid. If you see a slight mark left by the wake of your finger, it is ready to pour. Pour the slurry at a moderate speed into the base of your tile, trying hard to avoid splashing, which will cause air to get trapped beneath. The goal is to allow the plaster to fill the mold from the bottom up, covering the tile and driving out any air that might otherwise become trapped beneath the plaster **(2)**. Once all the plaster is used up, it

Note: Read the sidebar on page 70 for more information on plaster, including important safety precautions.

3

should be about 2" (5 cm) deep. Set the bucket aside to dry. Gently tap the underside or edge of the table for 1 to 2 minutes in a rhythmic fashion to agitate the plaster and send any trapped bubbles to the surface while the plaster is still in its liquid state. Let the plaster sit. Water will rise to the surface, then become absorbed, and the plaster will begin to heat up **(3)**. All of this is normal. Once the plaster has heated and cooled (about 20 to 30 minutes), you can unclamp and remove the cottle boards, flip the mold over, and remove the

tile from the mold. Shave down the edges of the mold with a rasp to round them out a little, which will prevent chipping when making and removing tile. Next, use a sponge and aggressively wipe down the mold in a bucket of clean water to clean and smooth it down. Let the mold sit overnight in a warm dry area so that it dries completely. Once dried out, it is ready to use.

Plaster

Plaster can be used for making simple one-piece molds, and incredibly complex multipart molds. Plaster's unique capillary properties allow it to remove the water from clay right away, which permits the clay to set up quickly and be removed in a relatively short amount of time. However, there are some precautions that must be taken when both mixing and using plaster with clay.

Plaster can be harmful to your lungs when breathed in as a powder in the making stage. It must be mixed in an open, well-ventilated space, and you must wear a respirator or filter mask to avoid inhalation of the harmful dust. Finally, wear latex gloves when mixing plaster as it is a caustic material that when wet can dry out and irritate your skin.

Plaster and clay make poor bedfellows when fired. If a piece of plaster gets caught in the clay and is fired, it will become embedded and present a problem when it absorbs the ambient moisture in the air. The plaster will swell to a degree that it can cause "popouts" that will ruin your finished piece.

Discard any clay that has been contaminated with plaster bits and any used for the mold-making process.

To properly mix plaster for mold making, you must have the proper proportions of water to plaster. If you try to eyeball your ratios, you will find it is never accurate and can lead to molds that are either too weak and spongy or too hard and brittle. You can also go down the rabbit hole of online debates on ratios, but I have found that the best resource for ratios is the U.S. Gypsum Corporation downloadable plaster calculator that can be found at www.plaster.com/consistency-calculator. The calculator is an Excel spreadsheet that takes out any guesswork and allows you to mix any volume of plaster perfectly every time!

A reminder that for this tutorial you are making a tile that is 4" × 4" × ½" (10 × 10 × 1.3 cm), and I have already provided the correct ratios of plaster to water: 2.8 lb (1.27 kg) of pottery plaster to 2 lb (0.9 kg) of very cold tap water.

Using a Tile Mold

If you've completed your tile mold or purchased a premade plaster mold for tile, you are ready to make tile with this tutorial. If not, turn back to page 65 to find the information you'll need to make a custom tile mold. On the following pages, you'll learn how to use your mold to create tiles out of clay.

Tools and Materials

- tile mold(s)
- ¾ lb (0.3 kg) of clay per tile, with each unit rolled into a ball
- rubber mallet
- 6" × 6" × ¾" (15 × 15 × 2 cm) wooden board
- 18" × 24" (45.7 × 61 cm) drywall board for placing finished tiles
- cut-off wire
- wire rack

Instructions

With the tile mold upright on a table, place a ¾ lb (0.3 kg) ball of clay in the cavity of the mold. Use your palm to press the clay into the mold as best you can. Place the wooden board on top of the clay and strike it with the mallet multiple times to compress the clay evenly throughout the mold. Remove the board and use the cut-off wire to remove excess clay from the top of the mold. Using the edge of the wooden board, scrape the top of the clay so that it is level with the top of the mold. Allow the mold to sit for a few minutes. The plaster will begin to remove some water from the clay, which should allow it to release from the mold **(1-4)**.

Cover the tile with your hand and flip the mold upside down. The tile will likely not come out, but if it does, great! Place the tile on the drywall board and start again. If the tile does not come out, hold the mold about ½" (1.3 cm) above the drywall and gently tap its edges with the rubber mallet. This should release the tile from the mold and onto the board. Repeat this process as many times as you can until the mold is too saturated with water to release the tile.

When not using the mold, leave it on a wire rack until it has fully dried.

1

2

3

4

Making a Set of Adjustable Cottle Boards

Tools and Materials

- four 12" × 4" × ⅝"
  (30.5 × 10 × 1.5 cm)
  wooden boards

- four 1" × 4" × ⅝"
  (2.5 × 10 × 1.5 cm)
  wooden boards

- four ¾" (2 cm) wood screws
- drill
- four 3" (7.5 cm) clamps

Instructions

The best tool for making a custom tile mold is a set of four cottle boards that can be adjusted to make molds of various sizes. These boards act as a dam that holds the wet plaster in and around the tile when casting. This particular set can be adjusted to cast objects that are up to 9" (23 cm) wide and 2" (5 cm) deep.

To make the cottles, start with four straight 12" × 4" × ⅝" (30.5 × 10 × 1.5 cm) wooden boards that have been sealed against moisture, and four 1" × 4" × ⅝" (2.5 × 10 × 1.5 cm) smaller pieces of the same wood. Add a light and even coat of wood glue to the 1" (2.5 cm) surfaces of each of the smaller pieces of wood. Affix the glued surface of each of the smaller pieces to the end of the long face of each of the larger boards. Make sure that each small piece lines up flush with its larger board so that there are no overhanging edges. Use the 3" (7.5 cm) clamps to hold each set together until they can be screwed in place.

Drill a pilot hole through the smaller piece and halfway into the larger board so that you can add a ¾" (2 cm) wood screw

to hold the two pieces together while they dry. Remove the clamps and let these sit overnight. You should now have four 12" (30.5 cm)-long boards that look like an elongated letter L with a small base.

To use these adjustable boards, place the 12" (30.5 cm) edge of one down on the table so the 4" (10 cm) edge is upright. Butt the other board in a similar manner against the end where the previous board meets to form its L. The small piece of the L is always the outside of the mold. Use the 3" (7.5 cm) clamp to bind the two boards together gently, clamping the face of one board to the L of the other. (The leg of the L should always be on the outside of the box you are forming.) Repeat these steps until you have built a box with all four boards that is open on the bottom and top and loosely bound by the 3" (7.5 cm) clamps. To adjust this box, slide the boards in or out to attain the desired size of the square or rectangular for the mold. When satisfied with the size of the mold, tighten each clamp.

CHAPTER 3

Surface: Glaze, Decoration, and Firing Tile

Surface treatment is the most researched and revered element of the entire ceramic tiling process. Surface decoration, while complex, is also what makes ceramic tile so significant. It is the fingerprint that gives clues to a tile's lineage. In the same manner that we may be rendered speechless by a mosque laden with intricate Persian tile or the allure of a satin glaze, tile speaks to our most basic instincts and unconsciously draws us in.

Deciding on glazes and slips, patterning, color choice, and other surface options can lead to a lifetime of discovery. I hope I offer you enough information to whet your appetite and take you down a path of deeper inquiry. In this chapter, I share a few intriguing ideas and surface design techniques for tile, ranging from slip decoration to complex forms of stenciling and glaze applications in hopes that they spark your curiosity. I also provide ways to test your surfaces to help in determining the best applications for your tile.

Use this chapter as a doorway to playful exploration of surface techniques and to develop your own voice through trial and error.

Surface

Surface is everything with tile. Patterned or blank, matte or glossy, colorful or earthy, glazed or unglazed, whatever your choice, you should get to know how a tile's surface speaks for itself and in conversation with its surroundings. Tile is meant to be enjoyed as well as used; it is equal parts form and function.

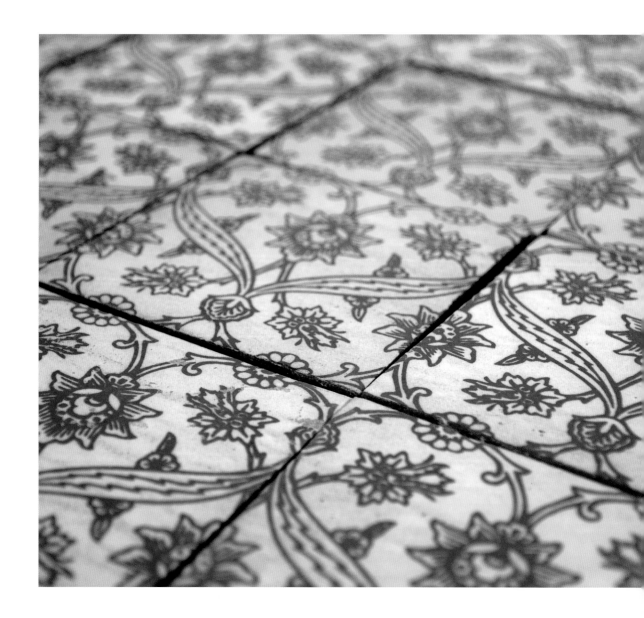

Relief tile by Blue Slide Art Tile. Photography by Laura Flippen.

GLAZED TILE

Glaze often provides the beauty and the intrigue of the surface. Glaze is to tile as gemstones are to jewelry. Humans are greatly attracted to shiny objects, and glaze—with all of its luster and fascination—is the perfect eye candy.

Glaze is also useful as a sealer for tile. Clays that have absorption rates of 1.5 percent or higher, such as earthenware, benefit greatly from the right glaze. Although glaze will not completely prevent an unvitrified tile from absorbing liquids, it goes a long way to mitigate localized staining and penetration of liquids.

Where functionality is concerned, it is good to know your tile inside and out. Poor-fitting glazes will affect the strength and functionality of both the glaze and the tile itself. This is exceedingly important to be aware of for unvitrified clays that need a reliable glaze to remain durable and easy to clean for years. Think about your tile as the body and your glaze as clothing. The right fit is incredibly important! You wouldn't purchase a jacket or pair of shoes without first trying them on, and you shouldn't make a batch of tile without first testing to ensure your glaze is compatible with your clay.

When applied at room temperature, glaze penetrates the clay's surface, bringing fluxing materials with it. When fired, the blending of glaze and clay can form a volatile and important flux, a third layer below the glaze and above the clay that is neither purely clay nor glaze, but a hybrid membrane called the interface. The interface layer plays a remarkable role that can help to develop a stronger tile—one that is less porous and essential for glaze fit, thus strengthening the tile.

Why bother testing? If your glaze has a thermal expansion that is considerably lower than your clay, it could end up shivering (flaking off). If the expansion is considerably higher, it could end up crazing, leaving tiny cracks that could compromise the tile by making it more vulnerable to the elements. Not all glazes are created equal: some that may appear durable could actually be quite soft, and vice versa. Always check to see that your glaze is durable upon your tiles' surface by glazing a few with your intended glaze and running some of the tests mentioned later in this chapter.

UNGLAZED TILE

Although you may think the vast majority of tile you encounter is glazed, that's not necessarily the case. Glazed tile is more resistant to staining and forms less patina due to its glassy topcoat. Also, because of the protective qualities of the glaze on a tile, there is a far wider range of ceramic tile that is glazed. However, for a host of functional, visual, and financial concerns, many makers choose to leave tile unglazed.

One of the questions I get asked most frequently is whether my own tile is glazed. It is not. There are pros and cons to unglazed tile that may be worth exploring. Color and surface are pillars of the design world, and unglazed tile can provide aspects of both that are unachievable with glazed tiles. Unglazed tile has high friction and traction properties, which can make it a good choice for wet areas, such as laundry rooms, bathroom floors, and outdoor spaces where high levels of moisture can create a slipping hazard. Commercial unglazed tile, such as quarry tile, is also more scratch resistant than glazed tile as it is typically made from durable high tech clays and has no glassy layer atop its surface to scratch. Finally, unglazed tile can prove to be the more economical choice to make, as there is no need for a glaze layer that requires a second firing.

Make sure to test and research the durability of handmade tile when you are not covering it with a protective glaze. An ill-fitting slip design can be beautiful, but it will be laid to waste if the design material is not durable enough. Be upfront with customers and inform them about the wear and tear properties of what you have to offer. Design work on an unglazed surface can be more vulnerable to wear than its glazed counterpart, as the often-thin design layers don't have a glaze surface to protect them. For example, the intention of my tile is that it eventually feels timeworn; it is unglazed and designed to wear slowly over time, adding a patina that looks natural. To clients who wish to mitigate these effects, I recommend a sealer that renders the surface more durable to foot traffic, which will prolong the "new" feel of the tile.

My 400% Asia tile set against white glazed tile from Fireclay Tile forms a wonderful contrast of materials.

Gordon Bryan, Blue Slide Art Tile

What defines handmade tile to you?

Handmade tile should show the hand of the maker: that could be in the cutting of the tile's shape, the edging of the greenware, or of course the glazing of the tile. These are all areas where the human hand can have an impact on the final product, whether that means a fingerprint, a dinged edge, or a beautiful brushstroke. The beauty is when those human marks work together harmoniously and with a degree of knowledge and intention.

What is the role of handmade tile in a world of mostly manufactured tile?

Every day we are surrounded by more and more "things" made without human touch. I'm talking about that hard, perfect edge, or a perfectly flat, square form. These things are cold; they aren't part of our makeup and they are rarely seen in nature. Handmade tile, on the other hand, reflects back on the observer or user. Rather than making us feel small or alienated, handmade tile helps us feel like part of our environment. It's made by and for another person, it shows that there is beauty in imperfections and variability—just like every one of us.

How much does your process inform your aesthetic?

My process and my aesthetic are inseparable. The tiles I make look the way they do because of the tools I use to make them. There are faster, cheaper, and more profitable ways to make tile, but I make them this way because I find beauty in the results. I could use a machine to make more uniform bisque, and glazing techniques that result in a more uniform surface, but there are huge factories that make much better flat, uniform tiles much cheaper than I ever could. What I have to offer are my hands, my eyes, and inspiration from where I live.

What has allowed you to be successful, and is there anything you can say that would be helpful to someone starting out?

That's a hard one to answer because you would have to define success. Most of us define it financially, but it's really about something deeper than that. I'm a maker; I need to be making things with my hands and that's one of the primary reasons I do what I do. I love making beautiful things, being independent, and exploring new ideas. If I had advice about starting and maintaining a tile business, the most important part would be about intent. After that, there are all the technical and business considerations. If I can offer one practical suggestion, it would be to complete an apprenticeship first. There's so much to learn and so many mistakes to make. You can easily shortcut the process by learning from someone else's successes and mistakes.

1 Songbird deco, hand-pressed tile; **2** Pond deco, hand-pressed tile; **3** Osprey, hand-carved tile; **4** Pines deco, hand-pressed tile; Photography by Laura Flippen

Surface: Glaze, Decoration, and Firing Tile

Testing Your Clay and Glazes

Each clay has its own unique properties. They vary in color, durability, and level of vitrification. My clay, for instance, has a broad firing range, and with each one I can expect a different fired result. I also fire with a unique schedule that could potentially affect the clay's vitrification and shrinkage across many parameters. Because of this, I have tested the clay I use with the three simple tests below. If you intend to have long-lasting tile that functions properly, you should do the same.

Note: When possible, run the three tests on the following pages against a tile that you know to be durable. This will give you a control to discern another tiles' durability.

TEST BARS

Prior to testing, you'll want to make ten to twenty test bars. This is quite an easy task, but when done with attention to detail and clear note-taking, it will allow you to understand your clay, glaze, and tile much better.

To make test bars, roll out a slab of clay that is the same body and thickness as the tile you will be making. The slab should be large enough to cut a number of 1" × 6" (2.5 × 15 cm) strips. After cutting the bars, while they are still wet, mark a 4" (10 cm) line down the center with a pointed tool, parallel to the length of the bar. Next, at each end of the carved line, mark perpendicular end lines like bookends to the main 4" (10 cm) line. These bars will be used for your clay's dry shrinkage, fired shrinkage, water absorption, and glaze hardness tests, so it is important that they are each identical, and the long line down the middle be exactly 4" (10 cm), otherwise you may foul your test results.

Shrinkage Test

Tile comes in many standard sizes: 3" (7.5 cm), 4" (10 cm), 6" (15 cm), and so on. It is absolutely paramount that you figure out the shrinkage of your clay so that you can target intended sizes with your clay throughout your line of offerings. Like absorption rates, the shrinkage that manufacturers list is relative to their own firing specifications.

Therefore, do your own shrinkage tests to gauge how your clay fires to your own parameters. Finding the shrinkage of your clay is quite simple. Immediately after making your test bars, dry them as you would any other tile, trying to keep them as flat as possible. Prior to firing, measure each bar's center line with a millimeter ruler and average the length to calculate how much your clay has shrunk. To do this, remember that each line was 4" (10 cm/100 mm); therefore, each millimeter of shrinkage accounts for a single percentage point. In other words, if your center line is now 94 mm, you have lost 6 percent going from wet to dry. Write this number down, recording it as your clay's wet-to-dry shrinkage.

Load your kiln as you normally would for bisque and disperse the bars throughout the stack. Fire and cool the kiln the way you normally would. Once it's unloaded, take a measurement of each center line and average your results. Though there is very little bone-dry to bisque shrinkage, you may find some. Write this down as bisque shrinkage. Finally, perform the same test for your final firing with multiple tiles dispersed throughout the kiln. This will not only show you what your relative shrinkage is, but it will also show you whether your kiln has fired evenly from location to location. Record the final number as your final shrinkage.

Absorption Test

Understanding the absorption of your fired clay body is key to the functionality and durability of your tile. The more your finished tile acts as a sponge, the weaker it can become from the eroding properties of water. This test should give you reliable results that pertain exactly to your tile. Just like with shrinkage, manufacturers will provide you with absorption rates for their clays, but they are usually only relative to a single temperature and firing schedule.

To test the absorption of your clay, run this simple test on any tile that has been fired to maturity.

Weigh at least three of the test bars by either grams or milligrams. Write down the weight and then place the tiles in a pot filled with water and make sure they are fully submerged. Set the pot to boil and leave the tiles in the water for exactly two hours. Once two hours have passed, let the water cool, remove the tiles, and pat them dry with a towel to remove all traces of standing water. Weigh the tile a second time. Note how much water weight each tile has absorbed and average them out. Compare the second number against the first by percentage and that will reflect the absorption rate of your tile. For example, if you tile weighed 100 grams before testing and now weighs 105 grams, you have an absorption rate of 5 percent.

Hardness Test

These glaze hardness tests are designed for dinnerware and smooth surfaces, yet they are also great for tile. They're a simple way to check whether you might need to either pick a new glaze or tweak your existing one to make it more durable. Though these tests are nonscientific and should not be intended as the authority, they are a good start to see whether your glaze will hold up under foot traffic and other rigorous circumstances.

Start by glazing and firing one of your test bars to maturity—or locate a standard tile that you have made with your intended clay and glaze. Once it's out of the kiln, use a sharp metal nail, awl, or screw and attempt to aggressively scratch the glaze's surface. You are checking to see whether holes develop in the glaze's surface or pieces of the glaze break off or crack. If this happens, you are penetrating the glaze's top layer and exposing its underlying surface. This shows that over time the glaze may wear down, especially if it's not sealed with a topical sealer.

Another simple test that is common for potters who make dinnerware is to see whether it "silver mars." To do this, use a fork or even a hacksaw blade to aggressively scratch the surface of the glaze. If the surface begins to show black or silver marks, attempt to scrub them away with soap and water. If they don't disappear, it can be a sign that your glaze is not as durable as you think.

Glazed tile by Blue Slide Art Tile. Photography by Laura Flippen.

Glazing

As glaze is an entirely different material from the clay itself, it should be no surprise that glaze is one of the most studied elements in the entire ceramic process. I recommend you take a workshop if one is offered at a ceramic studio near you, or check out one of the many great books devoted to the topic. (See page 201 for recommendations.) Because glaze formulation is such a complex and time-consuming part of our field, I will not go into great detail about material sciences here. Instead I will focus on options and techniques as they relate to tile.

COMMERCIAL GLAZES

There are entire stores dedicated to house paints: sometimes it can almost feel like the choice is made for you! Now imagine if you could walk into a ceramic supplier and get the same in-depth answers you are looking for when it comes to your glazes. Unfortunately it doesn't work quite that way. Increasingly reliable commercial glazes are available online and through your local supplier. Usually you won't get all the answers you are looking for in a commercial glaze, and each glaze's results will vary depending on the clay body it's on, exact firing temperatures, and atmosphere. However, the industry certainly has done a better job in recent years expanding its offerings and removing much of the guesswork. With some testing, you can begin to focus on what is most compatible with your aesthetic, your clay, and your studio capabilities.

There are some key things to be aware of when using commercial glazes. For instance, always know what your firing parameters are and work within them as a barometer for success. Read the labels and narrow down the glazes that fit within your target firing temperature and atmosphere, and test, test, test! Don't get lulled into thinking that because a glaze worked for someone else it will work for you. Also, even though these glazes were made by experts, they are not always the silver bullet solution.

HOMEMADE GLAZES

Just like cooking your own food, making your own glazes gives you more control over your results—yet the pursuit takes great commitment and attention to detail. Most industrial tile producers are dependent on consistent results, so they hire engineers to develop their glazes. You will find a split among many mid-level production tile makers. There are those such as myself, who choose to make their own glazes, while others employ the use of commercial glazes. Most low volume and project-based tile makers will simply use commercial glazes. Time, temperament, and cost are all things to consider when deciding whether to make your own glazes. If you are interested in trying this, see pages 198 and 199 for a few recipes.

Applying Glaze

Glazing is the most magnificent and mysterious element of the ceramic process. Witnessing the metamorphosis through firing is nothing short of astounding. Yet, if you're a potter, how many times have you come to the end of making something with clay only to be intimidated by the glazing process? As a material, glaze holds little of the immediate gratification that working with clay does. A piece of brittle bisqueware hardly compares to its malleable former self, and as such the glaze process represents an afterthought to many people. Rest assured though, many have cracked the code and found utter joy in glazing!

DIPPING

If you have experience glazing pottery, you'll find dipping glazes on tile can be just as quick and can yield the same great results. Because most tile is flat, you can simply hold it in your hand while dipping. Dip its face in the glaze by starting on one side, lowering the tile face in the glaze, and rocking it to the other side and out, making sure no air bubbles are stuck underneath. It's that simple. Keep an eye out for drips as you lift the tile out of the glaze. Fluid glazes can pool and drip toward one side as you are taking it out and setting it down to dry. Once all your tiles are glazed, inspect them with a critical eye, looking for drips that might have made it to the bottom edge of each tile.

Note: *You can use glaze tongs to dip tile, but often they can leave marks that will have to be rubbed away later. You will also have to wipe away or wash off the backs of the tile. Though I have seen some people wax the back sides of tile, it is not something I recommend as it adds cost and is time consuming.*

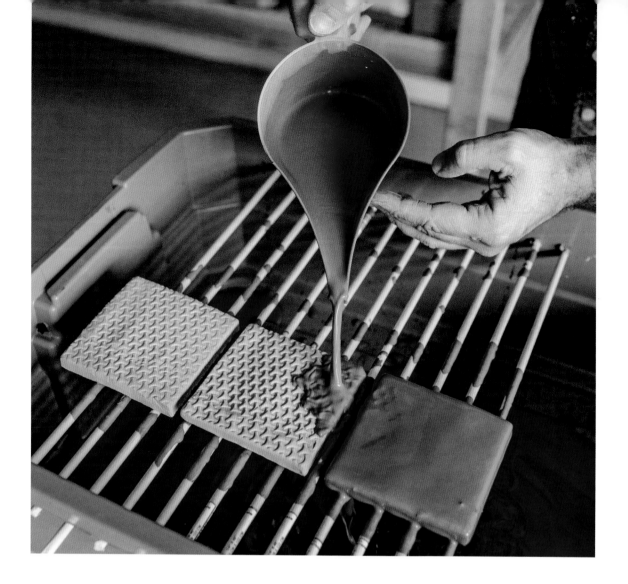

POURING/SPLASHING

Pouring, or splashing, glaze is a very reliable and common option used with handmade tile and, to a greater extent, in an automated industry setting. To glaze tile this way, fill a bucket with enough glaze so that you can scoop from it with a measuring cup or bowl. Lay each tile out in a line on a wire or wooden rack over the basin. Use a measuring cup to scoop some glaze and pour it over the bisqued tile in a left to right pouring motion. This should be done in a quick fashion while paying attention that you don't move so quick as to miss the upper left edge of the tile. The idea here is that the momentum of the fluid glaze should carry itself across the tile and provide an even coat.

Let the tiles dry, move them to the side, set more tiles on the rack over the basin, and repeat. Once you have glazed all of the tile, and after it has had enough time to dry to the touch, use a rubber scraper to scrape the edges of the tile back into the basin. After the tiles are scraped and the glaze is recaptured in the basin, use a damp sponge to clean the bottoms and edges of the tile. Although cleaning glaze can be tedious, this method of glazing can be quite rewarding.

PAINTING

Applying glazes with a brush can yield beautiful results that accentuate the handmade feel of tile. Painting directly on tile is a straightforward approach that can take time to master. When done correctly, it highlights surfaces and textures to great effect, humanizing the feel of the tile and making it quite approachable. I find that the best benefit with painted glaze is the use of localized blending of multiple glazes, where varied layers can be used to achieve stunning color and surface results.

Gordon Bryan applying glaze to a run of tile

Here my tips for painting glaze on tile:

- Layering can be quite complex. Make sure to test and track your glazes in combination with one another—glazes each have a unique chemistry that is developed for specific color, temperature, and surface results. Record which combinations run or change color, what defects you should avoid, and what effects you can exploit.

- Use natural fiber brushes, such as goat hair brushes, because they hold a great deal of glaze and are soft enough so as not to leave a mark.

- When brushing glazes, two coats are preferable for the base layer. The first coat will be absorbed quickly into the bisque-fired tile and the second will provide the thickness needed for the glaze. For an even glaze, first brush in one direction, let that coat dry, and then brush in the other direction to provide even coverage. After the base layers are dry, you only need one coat if you want to add another glaze or stain.

- Make sure to only paint the top surface of your tile unless it is a bullnose or edge tile that will be exposed. If you glaze the side of a tile, use a glaze that does not run, and clean it well with a sponge before firing to prevent it from sticking to the tile next to it, the shelf, or the stacker.

- Additives such as CMC gum or Veegum T (VGT) can be combined with glaze to aid with brushability and help keep glazes in suspension. They can also make applied glazes more durable once they have dried. If you know you will be brushing glazes, and you mix your own from dry materials, you can add about 2 percent VGT by weight to your dry mix. Give it about a day to set before you sieve so the VGT can absorb the water. If you don't want to mix entire batches with VGT as an additive, you can also keep a pint of VGT mixed with water to a gelatinous consistency on hand to be used with smaller batches of wet glaze. Use about 0.5 percent to 1.5 percent of the VGT gel by weight.

Note: *Many commercial glazes come with additives that aid in brushability. Test how your commercial glazes brush on before using additives.*

Wax and Latex Resists

Through the use of resists, you can achieve incredible layering and detailed glaze effects. Wax resist is the preferred glaze barrier as it stays in liquid form until it is applied. Wax resist is also much safer than paraffin wax, which needs to be heated to a liquid state and can create vapors that are a health hazard. Heating the paraffin can also lead to studio fires. You should avoid paraffin whenever possible.

Try adding 1 to 2 teaspoons (5 to 10 ml) of food coloring to 1 gallon (3.8 L) of wax resist to make it more visible when applied. You can also add water to wax resist so that it lasts longer. I add about 15 percent water to wax by volume until it is about the consistency of cream. Be forewarned though, watering wax down does make it a bit runny, and it can drip if it's too thin.

If you make a mistake with wax resist, leave the tile on top of a hot kiln or use a propane torch to burn it off. Test the area after it has cooled by adding a little water to the spot where the wax dripped and see whether it is absorbed or beads up. When the water is absorbed, the wax has been successfully removed. Wear gloves as bisqueware can become very hot to handle.

Latex resist is another option for layering glazes and slips. Latex is a paintable rubber resist barrier that can be used in the same fashion that you would use wax resist. What makes latex so unique is that it can be peeled off easily after it has dried, and then another coat of glaze can be added, and then latex, and on and on. Latex resist can unlock great potential for decorative applications!

SPRAYING

Spraying glaze is an incredibly common application in the industry. It is an ideal way to cover surfaces quickly and consistently and create otherwise unobtainable effects. However, for most artists, the proper safety equipment can be quite cost prohibitive and without it, overspray risks can cause potential health hazards from inhalation of airborne glaze. If you do spray your glazes, you will need to invest in an air compressor with a good regulator, a spray gun, a proper respirator, and a spray booth that can remove airborne glaze from your working environment. Here are my tips for successfully spraying tiles:

• Spraying is best done on bisque-fired tiles because they are absorbent and soak up glaze quickly, allowing for great productivity and consistent results.

• When spraying glaze, the tile should be placed on a wire rack or wooden dowels over a barrel to collect overspray and prevent the glaze from gathering or dripping at the bottom of the tile. (If dripping happens, it means cleanup later if you don't want the tiles sticking when fired.)

• Sprayed glazes should be watered down a little to flow properly through the equipment, and so that they don't layer too heavily.

• Spray your glazes from a distance of about 10" (25.5 cm) from the tile in a steady and consistent left to right motion. Try to move your spray gun in a flat horizontal motion parallel to the tile. Avoid making an arc with your arm as you spray as this could vary the distance from the tile, creating an uneven coat.

• Move at an even speed in each direction. Moving too quickly can create an uneven coat, and moving too slowly can create a runny surface. Either may be evident in the firing.

• Once you finish spraying a coat of glaze over the tile from left to right, rotate the tile or the gun 90 degrees and spray a second coat in a similar fashion so the tile has at least two even coats. This may sound time consuming, but remember that sprayed glazes dry almost instantaneously, and when spraying, you can coat multiple tiles at a time.

Decorative Ideas

Although glaze is the preferred method for sealing tile—and it can certainly stand alone as a design element—it is only a part of the decorative process. The majority of decorated tile that you see features some combination of glaze with other forms of decorative application. On the following pages are a few options for decorative techniques and materials that can be used when embellishing tile. I recommend choosing a single motif and trying each of these options to see which one works best with your tastes.

Bison and mouse tile by Mel Griffin. Photography courtesy of the artist.

OVERGLAZE

Using overglaze, also referred to as "on glaze," was once a common practice, but due to the success and ease of underglazes, as well as the fact that it is less durable, overglaze has fallen out of favor. One great advantage to overglaze is its sheer beauty. Though underglaze, for the most part, goes beneath the glaze and can become somewhat obscured, overglaze is applied on top of fired glaze and then refired at a very low temperature. Overglaze can be incredibly vivid and used to great effect—although usually on pottery and not tile.

Royal Vienna porcelain plate with an overglazed scene

DECORATIVE SLIPS

Decorative slips are the oldest form of added surface decoration on clay. Slip, a term often interchangeable with "engobe" (which is not quite the same thing), is simply liquid clay. It's often colored with pigments such as oxides and mason stains, and formulated to be pourable or paintable as a decorative element over wet and leather-hard clay. Traditionally slips were slaked down and often the heavier particles were separated, leaving the finest clays. These slips achieved a level of sheen and color differentiation when burnished that is unattainable any other way (such as terra sigillata). These slips also provided a modest form of sealant for the clay itself, and prior to the advent of glaze, they were commonly used for this purpose.

Colored slips are a fantastic option on so many levels. Because slips are clay, they are very compatible with wet clay and can be manipulated as such. For tile makers, slips provide a compatible surface decoration for many special effects, including slip trailing, sgraffito, mishima, marbling, brushwork, and color casting. These days, slips often play second fiddle to underglazes, as people are less likely to formulate their own materials, and because they don't have as wide of a range of application. As many artists have shown, however, colored slips have great value when used correctly.

Turiya Gross using paint slip on a greenware tile

UNDERGLAZE

As the name implies, underglazes are like decorative paints that are fired under a transparent glaze. Underglaze broke the decorative glaze spectrum wide open with the advent of the vibrant tile and wares that became synonymous with Islamic pottery and architecture. Underglazes have come a long way in the past twenty years. What used to be a few standard color and firing options have been fine-tuned by companies such as Amaco, Duncan, and Mayco to what seems like an endless assortment of reliable colors. Working with underglazes is now arguably the most user-friendly choice for decorating on clay. Underglazes are formulated to work with bisqueware, but they are also compatible with greenware, making them great for single firing, image transfer, wet work, mishima, sgraffito, and layering. Because fired underglaze colors are primarily "what you see is what you get," they are also great for blending to create other unique colors. Even if you never had any interest in working with underglazes, it is something I highly recommend everyone try. They are truly incredible products.

Applying underglaze can be quite easy with these helpful tips:

- Start with test tiles bisque fired to the manufacturer's specifications; tile fired too hot can be unabsorbent and lead to drippy applications that take too long to dry, while tile fired too low can absorb moisture too quickly and affect the quality of your brushwork.

- Test each underglaze tile in three sections: one with no cover glaze, one with a single coat of clear, and one with a double coat of clear. Save and use these test tiles like a sample library so that you can refer to them for predictable results on future projects.

- Clean your tiles with a damp sponge prior to application, as underglazes can be finicky when applied to dusty and oily surfaces.

- High quality natural hair brushes make a huge difference in application.

- Make sure to reload your brushes often for best results, and test for different results with multiple coats.

- Let each coat dry completely before applying the next coat or the underglaze may appear streaky.

Detail of Iznik tile

Detail of majolica tiles from the Cloister of Santa Chiara, Naples, Italy

IN-GLAZE

In-glaze is a method of applying stains colored with oxides, typically over a tin glaze that has been applied on bisque-fired earthenware and not yet fired. This unique decorative approach is particularly hard to master given that one must apply decoration over the glaze's chalky surface. In-glazed tile and pottery has a unique quality akin to a watercolor painting. As the thin wet stains are applied, they bleed just slightly. Like watercolors, different color values can be achieved by layering.

Once fired, these stains penetrate the glaze and add to the effect. This painterly effect has been exploited to perfection in many European tiles, such as the majolica earthenware so recognized with Italian ceramics and tile. Another example is the blue and white Delftware tile of the Netherlands. It was originally developed as an imitation of Chinese blue and white porcelain, then became so popular that the name Delft itself has become synonymous with anything blue and white!

Image Transfer: Printing on Clay

I remember being captivated the first time
I saw Paul McMullen magically add an image to
a slab of clay with the ease of a temporary tattoo.
It was my freshman year of college and I didn't
know it at the time, but I was witnessing the beginning of an image transfer renaissance brought
on by pioneers such as Richard Shaw, Philip
Cornelius, and Paul Scott. It would be further
developed through the use of technology and
inquiry in the tile industry and arts programs
throughout the world, and redefined by artists
such as Andy Brayman, Kristen Morgin, Lesley
Baker, and Paul McMullan.

Note: *I use a process for image transfer that is
virtually interchangeable for my pottery and tile.
Though my own innovations lie in the way I
apply a transfer to a volumetric wheel-thrown
pot, I must give credit to Richard Shaw and
Lesley Baker in particular.*

Tools and Materials

- prepared 20" × 24" (51 × 61 cm), 156 mesh count aluminum frame silk screen (See page 200 for ordering information.)

- 70 durometer squeegee, approximately 14" (35.6 cm)

- 2 hinge clamps

- table to mount the hinge clamps to or a portable 24" × 28" (61 × 71 cm) smooth surface board

- 1 pint (475 ml) of underglaze or image transfer medium (See recipes on page 199.)

- Super 77 spray adhesive

- 18" × 24" (45.5 × 51 cm) of 25- to 30-weight newsprint

- metal yardstick or tear bar

- rags

- rubber or plastic spatula or scraper

- 12" × 18" (30.5 × 45.5 cm) slabs of soft leather-hard clay

- 6" (15 cm) hake brush

- ½ gallon (3.8 L) of deflocculated transfer slip in a 1 gallon (3.7 L) bucket (See recipe on page 198.)

- flexible rubber rib (I prefer the yellow rubber rib from Mud Tools.)

- 18" × 20" (45.7 × 50.8 cm), or larger, piece of drywall

GETTING STARTED WITH IMAGE TRANSFERS

Image transfer has the potential to change your work in many ways. It is a complex process but, once learned, it can cut production times, add layers of surface imagery, and challenge one's understanding of modern ceramics. In this section, I explain my screen printing process as well as some variations that I have seen, used, and developed over time. While you can make your own silk screen and build your own exposure unit, it does require a modest investment in time and equipment, and so for this section I will not go into great detail on how to make a silk screen. The easiest way to get what you need for this tutorial is to order a pre-burned screen from one of the vendors in the Resources section (page 200). Alternately, you can find instructions on how to burn a screen, set up a screen printing jig, and more my website, www.flmceramics.com, or in a whole host of screen printing books that go into great detail on how to burn your own screens at home—I suggest starting with *Graphic Clay* by Jason Bige Burnett.

SETTING UP THE PRINT

Before using your screen, tape the edges with the screen block out to cover the gap between the emulsion and the frame where the emulsion did not reach. This process takes practice. Always tape the interior edge of the screen along the frame, and not the flat face or front of the screen. To tape the screen, cover from the edge of the emulsion to the frame and then bend the tape up the frame roughly ½" (1.3 cm). Your tape should make a 90-degree angle between the screen and frame and be stuck down with few to no creases or air bubbles. The best method I have found is to tape the top and bottom edges of the screen first, and then the long sides.

Next make sure that the hinge clamps are screwed down in place at the top of the board, or on the table, so that when the screen is in the down position it does not hang off the front **(1)**.

Place the silk screen frame into the clamps facedown; the frame itself should be facing up, and the mesh should be facing down. Secure the frame in place by tightening the thumbscrews. The screen should be able to lift up and down on the hinges and stay in place **(2)**.

Lift the screen to the upright position so that it stays up independently and spray the surface of the table or board with a light coat of the spray adhesive. Place the newsprint below the screen and on the board. Gently rub the newsprint so that it fully adheres to the board. Bring the screen to the down position. There should be roughly ⅛" (3 mm) clearance between the screen and the newsprint beneath it.

Spread a generous amount of image transfer medium onto the bottom edge of the screen mesh to form a well of printing medium about 1½" (4 cm)

from the bottom edge of the frame **(3)**. Place the squeegee in contact with the screen and parallel to the bottom of the frame with the print medium in front of the squeegee. From where you stand you should see the bottom of the frame, the squeegee, and the rest of the screen (the squeegee will be blocking your view of the print medium). Next, with one hand, lift the screen roughly 4" off the board and, holding the squeegee at an angle away from you with your other hand, use the weight of the squeegee to push the medium from the bottom of the screen to the top **(4)**. This is called a flood coat and it helps to ensure a good print by keeping the screen from drying out later. With the well at the top, you're ready to print.

Note: *It is important that when doing this you always maintain firm, downward contact between the squeegee and the board, with the paper in between.*

Relax your downward pressure so that the screen springs back up. Lift the squeegee up and set it down carefully, so as not to get the transfer medium anywhere you don't want it. Lift the frame upward on the hinges just high enough so that you can see whether your image printed. If the image only printed partially, repeat the process from top to bottom without flooding or adding more transfer medium. Your well should stay at the bottom of the screen closest to you. Lift again and check for a cleanly printed image **(5).**

Once you have printed the image, flood the screen again to keep the screen from drying out—it also loads the image for the next print. Once you have done your flood coat, the well of transfer medium should have moved back to the top of the frame. Leave the screen in the up position, lift off the printed paper carefully, and replace it with another. The spray adhesive will last for five to ten prints before it needs to be reapplied. You are now printing **(6)**!

Once your images have been printed, allow the paper to dry for about half an hour. Then tear or cut down the edges so all that remains is the printed part, and not the blank borders. I tear the paper down with a metal yardstick or tear bar. You can also cut away the borders with scissors if tearing it is too cumbersome.

TRANSFERRING PRINT TO CLAY

Now that you have an image printed on paper, here is where the magic begins. You will now take your image from two dimensions to three.

For your setup, begin with the printed and torn-down transfer, the ½ gallon (1.9 L) of deflocculated transfer slip, the hake brush, the 12" × 18" (30.5 × 45.7 cm) leather-hard slab of clay, the flexible rib, and the 18" × 20" (45.7 × 50.8 cm) piece of drywall.

Place your transfer on the sheet of drywall image side up, and the soft leather-hard slab on the table you will be working on. Using the hake brush,

paint the deflocculated slip directly on the leather-hard slab using even strokes to make sure that you don't create any pooling **(7)**.

Rewet your brush and paint an even coat of the slip on the printed side of the paper, making sure to get full and even coverage. (If your transfer begins to lift with the brush, hold the corner down with one hand and paint with the other.) Let the slip dry on the surfaces of the paper and slab for roughly 3 to 4 minutes so that they each become tacky to the touch and no pools of wet slip exist. Pick up the transfer and begin by gently placing one edge facedown on the edge of slab, slip-to-slip **(8–10)**.

Once the edge of the transfer has made contact with the edge of the slab, lay it down the rest of the way until the entire printed surface is in contact with the slab. Try not to trap air pockets or wrinkle the paper.

Use the rubber rib to smooth over the paper from the center outward, pressing down lightly and using the rib as a squeegee to ensure that the transfer and slab have made good contact. You are also pushing out any air bubbles and wrinkles that may have been trapped when the transfer was placed down **(11)**.

Peel up one corner of the transfer to check whether the image transferred to the slab. Be careful not to lift the entire transfer off, which will cause the transfer to lose registration. The image should transfer to the slab in a similar way that a temporary tattoo transfers to skin. If the image has not transferred, push the lifted edge back down and smooth over it again with the rubber rib while pressing and dragging with a little more pressure. Pull up the corner and peek again. Once you are satisfied with the results, slowly peel up the entire transfer to reveal the printed image on the slab in its entirety **(12-13)**.

Susanne Redfield, founder of Kibak Tile

Floor and backsplash, Riser 8 pattern. Designed by Karrie Trowbridge, Maker of Home. Photography by Gallivan Photos

What drew you to cuerda seca/dry line as a decorative technique?

Born and raised in Southern California, I was surrounded by the original Malibu tile and Catalina tile—tiles that were an integral part of the classic Spanish Colonial Revival architecture so common in coastal towns. My heroes in the ceramics world were Betty Woodman and Jun Kaneko, both pattern builders and colorists. In California, I was also exposed to the tile work of Barbara Vantrease Beall and Gemma Taccogna; their style was painterly, with a fearless use of color. I was also influenced by the precision and clean lines of Nordic design. Cuerda seca really lent itself to the crisp and minimalist style I appreciated. I found that the geometric patterns I was designing were really suited to the dry line style. Most important,

dry line was a technique that I could teach others. I was infinitely more interested in designing, manufacturing, and building a business than producing one-of-a-kind artwork.

Given that pattern is such an integral part of your work, what thoughts can you share about working with it?

I spent a lot of time growing up in Denmark; the aesthetics of its modern movement really had an impact on me. Everyday items were as functional as they were beautiful. One reason I think I turned my attention to tile in the world of clay was that tile is a necessary, common building material; it is simple, basic, and serviceable. Our home, in California, was decidedly Danish modern, including pieces by Hans Wegner, Kaare Klint, Arne Jacobsen, and Finn Juhl. I think I was introduced early to the notion that living with good design was important, even essential. Even our daily eating utensils were a mix of different Georg Jensen patterns, of which I definitely had my favorites, and I noticed design. I was drawn to the exuberance of Maija Isola and Marimekko. I was a huge Josef Frank, Svenskt Tenn fan, and when I discovered Bjørn Wiinblad, I was smitten with pattern for good.

What was your journey for selling and marketing your tile?

I have been in the tile business since 1981. I started my career selling tiles through Kneedler Fauchere, one of the finest, most exclusive interior showrooms in the country. Country Floors had just left to set up its own showroom and Dorothy Kneedler and Harry Lawenda were looking for

(continued)

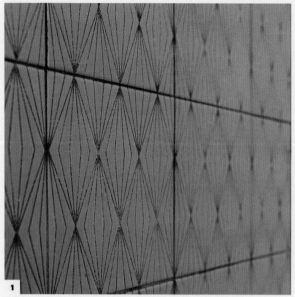

something special. I was thrilled to be picked, and they taught me so much about excellence and professionalism. Presenting my line to architectural firms such as Gensler and design giants like Hirsch Bedner was nerve wracking, but I soon learned that a good product speaks for itself, that honesty and integrity are what is important, and that developing good relationships are what make the work interesting. After a few years, I moved my tile lines to Daltile. In my opinion, it was better to be where people go to specifically buy tile than to be in a showroom where they are buying fabric, furniture, and lighting. I learned how to work with an industry leader, collaborated successfully in Dal's builders program nationwide, and hired more people. I grew from a studio to a factory. At the same time, I met Ann Sacks, a force of nature in the tile world, and started selling tiles through her stores in Portland and Seattle. When Ann sold her

business to Herb Kohler and expanded it, we grew along with the expansion. I loved the relationships I developed with the salespeople at Ann Sacks and found I prefer making tiles for a highly trained sales staff; it was inspirational and a pleasure working with such a talented group of people.

In 2014 I decided to switch it up again. I didn't want the responsibility of a factory forever so I downsized to a studio again, my daughter joined me, and we started making just what we wanted to make and selling to a few showrooms directly as well off a website and off Instagram. Today, instead of a half an hour commute each way, I can ride my bike less than a mile to a small studio in the Sisters industrial park. I make tiles with my daughter and work with friends who have been selling tile with me for decades. It's a sweet life!

1, 2 Floor and feature wall, Uni Diamond pattern. Interior design by Karrie Trowbridge, Maker of Home. Photography by Gallivan Photos. **3** Feature Wall, Sakura Cherry Tree mural. Interior design by Laurel Quint Interior Design. Photography by Emily Minton-Redfield.

Cuerda Seca ("Dry Cord")

The cuerda seca, or "dry cord," technique is something you may recognize from Middle Eastern and Spanish tile. Though the name is Spanish, it was most likely developed in Iran and brought to Spain during the Moorish period. Cuerda seca was developed to imitate the complexity of mosaics without the complex work that goes into setting mosaic tile. The genius of cuerda seca lies in the way glazes are compartmentalized throughout a single tile with relative ease.

To achieve this compartmentalization, a mixture of oil (or in some cases wax), pigment, and ceramic flux—such as manganese or iron—is laid down on a tile as line decoration. After drying, the pigment becomes a colored line decoration that is also an impermeable resist, keeping glazed sections compartmentalized from one another. Glazes are applied to individual areas by the use of a bulb syringe, or in some cases densely saturated brushes.

Tools and Materials

- 10 or more 6" × 6" (15 × 15 cm) bisque fired tiles ⅜" (1 cm) thick
- silk screen with a 6" × 6" (15 × 15 cm) geometric linework image

- pigmented cuerda seca medium in a squeeze bottle for printing with the silkscreen (See the recipe on page 199.)
- 8 ounce (237 ml) squeeze bottle-style applicators for each glaze you will be using

- several sheets of 18" × 24" (45.5 × 61 cm) 25- or 30-pound (37 or 44 gsm) newsprint
- Super 77 spray adhesive
- 2½" (6.4 cm)-thick strip of wood 2" (5 cm) wide × 16" (25.5 cm) long

- masking tape
- pencil
- cuerda seca print medium in the recipes section on page 199
- 70 durometer squeegee, approximately 14" (35.6 cm)

Note: *This tutorial assumes you have 6" × 6" (15 × 15 cm) tiles bisque fired to cone 06.*

Cuerda seca detail from Yesil Turbe (Green Tomb), Bursa, Turkey

1

Carli Strachan of Kibak applying glaze to tile with cuerda seca technique.
Photography courtesy of Kibak Tile.

PRINTING IMAGES TO TILE
FOR CUERDA SECA

Unlike the previous method of making a newsprint transfer, this printing method involves printing directly to tile, therefore you must first shim the screen to sit just above the height of the tile you will be printing on. To do this, sandwich one of the 1½" (3.8 cm)-thick strips of wood beneath the screen and above the hinge clamps. Now tighten the hinge clamps to hold the screen securely. It should look like the screen and wood are a sandwich with the clamps being the bread. Now when the screen is lowered, the mesh should rest about 1 to 2 mm above the height of the fired tile. Tape the other shim on the table where the close edge of the screen makes contact, so that when you lower the screen, the edge of the frame closest to you comes to rest on the shim when printing.

Spray a small amount of the adhesive on the printing table and set a piece of newsprint down in place beneath where the screen will be printing.

Lower the screen, slide a tile underneath, and center the tile under the image on the screen. Lift the screen and hold the tile in place. Outline the tile on the newsprint with a pencil, creating a rough registration mark for printing each tile.

Add a generous bead of the cuerda seca printing medium at the bottom of the screen that is the width of the image. Following the printing technique taught on pages 102 to 108, use your squeegee to flood and then print the image directly onto the tile. Lift the screen and flood it again. Check your tile to see whether your registration is correct. If it is not registered properly, adjust the tile slightly to make sure the screen is on target, redraw the registration, and test it again until it is centered. Once registered to your liking, you are off to the races! Place the next tile in the registration, lower the screen, and run the next print. Once you have printed all tiles, let them dry for a full twenty-four hours before glazing **(1)**.

Notes: *Your glazes should be sieved and thinned enough so that they flow from the syringe smoothly. If your glaze is too thin, it could run over the grease-pigment dam, and if it is too thick, it may clog and squirt out all at once, creating a mess on your tile that will be hard to clean up. You need to develop a glaze that is the right consistency for your process.*

This process can also be done without the use of a silk screen. To do so, simply use a fine tip paintbrush or bulb syringe to paint your pigmented grease medium freehand. This technique works great for murals where the image covers the entirety of the space rather than a single repetitive tile tessellation.

Carli Strachan of Kibak applying glaze to tile with cuerda seca technique.
Photography courtesy of Kibak Tile.

2

GLAZING CUERDA SECA TILE

The glazing process is where the magic of cuerda seca comes to life. Once the pigmented grease has been allowed to set for 24 hours, set the tile on a table or banding wheel. You can map out your colors ahead of time, or you can work freehand depending on your style and level of detail. Choose a single glaze color in a bottle with a needle tip to start with and shake it well, making sure to cover the tip of the needle so glaze doesn't come out. Pick a section within the pattern to start with and apply the glaze to the interior edges of that section by tracing the border of the printed image all the way around and then filling inward as if you were creating a little pond of glaze that uses the printed line as a dam. If done correctly, the glaze should stay within the grease dam, and the surface tension of the glaze should make it stand up quite a bit higher than the tile's surface. Within a minute or so the glaze should begin to soak in and dry up, reducing in volume and holding its place. Do not agitate the tile as the glaze is drying **(2)**.

As you are glazing, you may create an air bubble in your glazed area, or where the glaze doesn't run into the edge of the dam well. If this is the case, gently drag the tip of the applicator bottle through the dry spot (or bubble) and let the glaze fill it in, or lift up the edge of the tile a couple of millimeters and tap it on the table or banding wheel to coax the glaze into the right spot.

Once you have completed each of the spaces that require your first color, move to the next color and so on until the tile is completed. Let your glaze dry, and fire it as you would any other tile.

Plaster Transfer

Plaster transfer is a unique method of getting
an image with fine detail on to a slab or tile with
underglazes. Like cuerda seca, plaster transfers
can be done by screen printing or painting a
monoprint image directly onto the plaster. Here
I will show the screen printing method, but you
could do the same by painting underglaze on the
plaster as a monoprint transfer.

Tools and Materials

- 18" × 20" (45.5 × 51 cm)
  slab of plaster that is as
  smooth as possible
- custom silk screen
  ordered from
  page 200
- 70 durometer
  squeegee
- underglaze

- 1 pint (475 ml) of
  casting slip
- 4" (10.2 cm) leather-
  hard tiles (optional)
- wooden knife tool (or
  wood clay knife)
- 5 lb (2.3 kg) of clay
- tile cutter/pizza cutter/
  fettling knife

1

2

This project shares some elements with the tutorial beginning on page 103, but instead of applying your transfer medium (underglaze or slip) to newsprint, you will print your image directly on a clean and smooth plaster slab using underglaze. Lay the silk screen directly on the plaster and use the squeegee to apply a single layer of underglaze through the screen onto the plaster **(1-2)**.

Because plaster is like a sponge, make sure to lift the screen off the plaster soon after printing or it may stick and clog the screen **(3)**.

With the image on the plaster slab, use clay coils or cottle boards to build a ½" (4 cm)-high dam around the image to act as a reservoir. Once in place, shore up the bottom edges of reservoir with a final clay coil sealed tightly between the reservoir and cottle boards all the way around to prevent it from leaking **(4)**.

There are two pouring options for making a transferred tile. The first is to pour the slip to the thickness that you would like for your tile, and then let it sit for about 30 to 60 minutes, until the slip feels firm enough to release from the slab. Remove the dam and begin to gently peel up the edges of the slip to test whether it is ready to come off easily. If it feels loose from the slab, begin to peel up the slab completely and reveal the image. Place the clay image side up on a table and cut out the size and shape of tile you'd like with a tile cutter, pizza cutter, or fettling knife **(5)**.

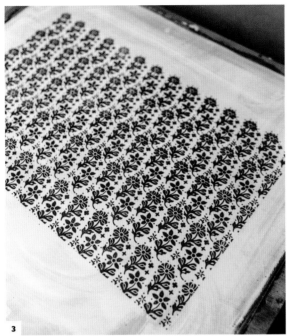

3

4

5

The second option is to create a thin veneer that will be laminated on top of the tile. You will need a leather-hard tile that has a compatible shrinkage and firing rate to your slip. Pour the slip on top of the plaster slab to no more than 1 to 2 millimeters thickness. While the slip is still wet, place the leather-hard tile (or tiles) on the slab. Let them sit for thirty to sixty minutes, until the veneer has stuck to the tile and they both begin to release from the plaster slab together as one piece. Carefully cut around the tile and through the slip veneer with the wooden knife, making sure not to damage the plaster slab. By now the tile should be ready to lift up with the slip veneer and turn over, revealing a cleanly laminated image on top of the tile. Let the two sit and dry slowly to make sure that the veneer doesn't pull away from the tile.

Firing

Like drying, firing is a step that can easily lead to the success or failure of your tile. Unloading a kiln can be a complete joy, or a frustration beyond compare. Warping, discoloration, and cracking are common problems that arise when firing tile. Read this section for some tips that can help to ensure the success of your next firing.

STACKING

How you stack a kiln with tile is extremely important. There are many ways to stack a kiln, but the goal is always the same: get as much tile into the kiln as possible, while still being able to maintain an even temperature and atmosphere throughout the firing cycle. From complicated refractory stacking systems to simply setting tile on flat shelves, the goal is to stack in a way that prevents warping and cracking. Unlike with pots, tile loads can be repeated almost exactly the same way for each firing because tiles are usually a consistent size. Keep a good kiln log that chronicles the loading, unloading, and firing process to cut down on variables and isolate any problems that occur with relative ease. This will allow you to achieve consistent repeatable results and turn over the firings in a more efficient manner.

The best kiln furniture for tile is usually something that allows for stacking the tiles in relatively close proximity to one another to save space and create even heat distribution. Some tile stackers are slotted and open on the bottom, and some are like miniature kiln shelves that stack. In cases where sticking glaze isn't a concern, and when working with unvitrified clays, it is even possible to "tumble stack" tiles on top of one another. I fire my own tile in tile stackers that hold between eighteen to twenty-two tiles depending on the size of the tile I am firing.

In many cases, it is best to leave the stackers in the kiln, unloading and reloading them in place when possible. This saves time and cuts down on breakage that can occur from moving stackers. It can also help prevent the stackers from warping.

The most common cause of cracking is uneven heat. When loading tile, try to place them in a manner that keeps them from being too close to the heat source, be it a kiln element or open flame. I suggest that tile be at least ½" (1.3 cm) from an element, or 1" (2.5 cm) from a flame path.

David Dick and Krista Schrock,
DISC Interiors

Can you briefly describe how you view your role as designers?

DISC Interiors creates custom homes for clients by designing kitchens, interior architectural details, bathrooms, and even custom furniture. We also select decorative works such as lighting, cabinets, hardware, rugs, tiles, artwork, and so on, sourcing many of them from local studios.

Our role as interior designers is to create meaningful spaces and homes for our clients, and also to capture their personality and desires for living in a physical space. We believe in collaborating with our clients throughout the process and translating initial bits of inspiration and creative sparks into a full design. In creating custom homes, we strive to pull the clients' personal stories into the work, whether that is color, materials, space planning, or specific pieces of furniture.

David, as someone who worked as a craftsman for some time, and has since accomplished a very successful design career, how would you describe the ideal relationship between craft and design, as well as makers and designers?

In my early twenties, when I blew glass and focused on producing decorative sculptural works, I formed a partial understanding of what life is like when one is dedicated to their own craft. It gave me not only a look into how a craft studio works and operates, but also a large amount of respect for those who work and create with their hands.

It allowed me to appreciate the marks of the craftsperson, and to understand the difference between commercial production and truly artisanal work. Both have their place and the balance between the two can be remarkable.

When blowing glass and pursuing craft as a profession, I had not yet discovered the world of interior design and residential architecture. I also did not fully understand the larger picture of how craft can interact in that world and play such a vital role. At that time, I was dedicated to "the object," and to the history of objects, but I had not yet discovered how one artist's objects can work with objects from other artists and designers, all working together to create something larger. (There is a book called *The Unknown Craftsman* by Bernard Leach, which captures these ideas.)

Tile is found everywhere and is often easily overlooked. How can you describe the use of tile within your work and can you share some ways you might use it on a project?

DISC uses tiles in kitchens as backsplashes, feature walls in homes, fireplaces, exterior and interior applications, staircase risers . . . and anywhere else we can think of! The material of clay is a material we are drawn to as designers, as it has a sense of history, permanence, and natural beauty. We love the various glazes and the ability that handmade tile has to cast light and shadows around a room.

1 Kitchen backsplash, detail, FLM Ceramics Alborz tile; **2** Shower, handmade Zellige tiles; **3** Kitchen backsplash, FLM Ceramics Alborz tile; Photography by D. Gilbert

Understanding Tile in the Context of Your Home

Traditionally tile was used in the hot and dry climates of the Middle East, North Africa, Mexico, the American Southwest, and the Mediterranean, where it embodied a perfect balance of both form and function. The history of these places, and their design aesthetics, has most influenced the use of tile in a modern context. In hot climates, nothing beats solid earth for moderating indoor temperatures. Homes made of clay, brick, rammed earth, and stucco keep buildings warm in the winter by storing heat in their thick walls. They also remain cool in the summer by maintaining a constant temperature as an extension of the earth below.

As building materials developed, fired terra-cotta tile and brick replaced many of the unfired earth structures. Tile and brick have similar heat retention and cooling properties, yet are more durable, water resistant, and require less material and support than unfired earth. Add the advent of decorative slips and glazes and you have a perfect material that integrates form and function. Once perfected, fired earthenware became the natural choice for roofing and skinning buildings, and along with stoneware and porcelain tile, it still is used widely to this day.

As globalized trade developed, so did the market for porcelain and stoneware tile. With the development of European porcelains and stoneware, along with the advent of the East Asian tile market, an endless array of materials and new tile designs took hold. Stoneware and porcelain are the modern standard for floor tile because they are more durable than their earthenware cousin. Although the prices for porcelain and stoneware tile are higher because of firing and material costs, it is often worth the price when considering the durability, color range, and longevity they provide for flooring (although it is hard to beat the visual warmth of terra-cotta tile).

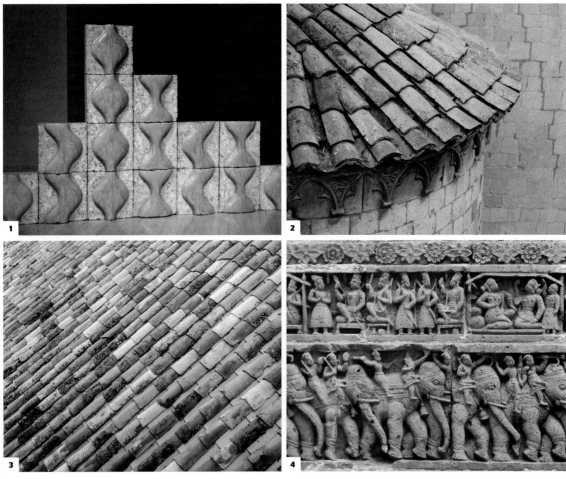

1 *Wall Number 4* by Jason Green; photography courtesy of the artist **2** Tiled roof, Dubrovnik, Croatia
3 Terra-cotta tiles on a rooftop in Toledo, Spain **4** Architectural terra-cotta tiles, Kantajew Temple, Bangladesh

In the modern-day home, tile is often the best solution for a handsome backsplash or shower, as well as a floor in a room such as the kitchen or bathroom. This is because tile is incredibly easy to clean, it doesn't stain easily, and it requires very little maintenance. Tile is also hypoallergenic and does not attract or trap pet hair or dirt like carpet does. Be forewarned, however, tile should not be a spur-of-the-moment choice; it takes a commitment to proper planning and care, and high-quality handmade tile can be expensive. Once installed, tile is permanent and hard to salvage. If you choose to make changes with tile, you will have the added concern of pulling it up (see page 170).

KITCHEN AND BATH TILE

For kitchens and baths, choose tile that is vitrified and glazed, or at least sealed properly so that it is impervious to spills and splashes. Kitchen and bath tile must not be absorbent because if it can absorb moisture, it can also absorb soap scum and grease, making it impossible to clean properly. Absorption of liquid can also affect the durability of the tile. As moisture penetrates, it can grow bacteria. It is necessary to seal kitchen and bath tile that is earthenware, and the grout as well. Although the firing process for most tile is very consistent, and quality is almost assured, there is always the possibility of an errant tile that may not be fully vitrified, especially in the case of hand-made tile. Because of this, many people suggest sealing even when the manufacturer claims the tile is vitrified.

FLOOR TILE

Floor tile is a challenge, to say the least! Many of my favorite commissions have been floors. These installations require unique parameters. Floor tile needs to be flat and durable, as well as slip-, stain-, and wear-resistant. Most important, floor tile must be installed properly. No other tile application requires the scrutiny of floor tile. Add to this the vast quantity of tile needed for floors, and the ability to bring a room together visually, and you can make or break a project with floor tile.

The most common floor tile is quarry tile. Though it sounds like it is stone and cut from a rock quarry, it is not. Quarry tile is large-scale unglazed tile. Often textured, it embodies everything a floor tile should be, except for one thing—it is usually quite uninteresting. For that reason, you often find quarry tile in areas where aesthetics are not important. Aside from quarry tile, another option is porcelain floor tile because of its durability and high level of vitrification. Terra-cotta tile used to be a standard in many places, and it is often more affordable, yet terra-cotta is a softer clay and wears down much quicker.

Custom Asia fireplace tile by FLM Ceramcis, Mill Valley, California. Photography by Allison Bloom.

a space and calculate what quantity of tile to use, how to work within a budget, and even how to find the contractors who will best install your tile. The best designers can make your idea even better than you thought it could be without minimizing your vision.

When it comes to getting my tile into the hands of a customer, I primarily work with designers. Designers manage multiple projects at any given time; if a job arises where they see my tile will be a good fit, they ask me for samples to share with the client. If the client approves, the designer contacts me for lead times. For my tile, a standard lead is about six to eight weeks.

Once we have a verbal agreement, the designer sends a purchase order and I provide an invoice for the job with an estimate on shipping. (Shipping rates vary and an exact price cannot be guaranteed more than a week or so out.) When the deposit is paid, I begin the job. After the deadline or the completion of the job, I provide an actual shipping cost, and the designer or the client pays the balance of the invoice plus shipping. When final payment is received, I box and palletize the tile, and the shipping broker sends a truck. Once shipped, I provide a tracking number to the designer and client, and the job is in the hands of the shipping fairies and the tile setter.

Most designers tell me that their favorite part of their job is being out in the world picking out objects and surfaces and building those relationships. A designer can take everything they know and apply it to your tile, and then apply that to the space as a whole. They know how to assess

Allison Dehn Bloom

How would you describe your role as a designer?

I am the channel. The goal is always to create a welcoming, beautiful home that reflects the family who lives there. I translate a family's values, tastes, and dreams into a physical space. This means that no two of the homes I do are alike. One of the joys of the job is finding new makers and artisans to reflect each family's aesthetics and home life.

What are the qualities that you look for and what intrigues you most about tile?

So much of a home is linear surfaces: walls, floors, and ceilings. These are often homogenous (one paint color, one floor stain, and so on). A welcoming and cozy home is created out of the interplay between texture, pattern, and color. Tile brings all three and imbues a home with a sense of history and permanence.

Describe the ideal client or project.

The ideal client knows who they are and what they want their home to be about. They also trust me to be the vehicle for that artistic expression of their personality.

Speaking directly to the maker, what can you say that may be helpful in their pursuit of breaking into the world of home design and decor?

Have something to say with your work. People respond to why you do things, as much as they respond to what you are doing. A sense of soul comes through when a product exists because the maker has something to say with their work—or a point of view or aesthetic they want to communicate.

How do you build relationships within the field and what can you say that might be helpful for others (artists, designers, and even installers)?

Everyone responds to genuine appreciation of their work. That is the first step. I think most relationships—and businesses—boil down to how you treat people. I always lead with kindness, and I believe most people try their best. In an industry where nearly everything is custom, there are many opportunities for things to go sideways, and they often do. Where things go from there is key: having a foundation of genuine respect and following it with kindness and fairness in your interactions is paramount. For makers, this means being upfront about any delays, surprises, or mishaps, and working together with us to find a solution. Sometimes mistakes lead to the best final products!

1 Heath tile backsplash, San Francisco. Photography by Daniel Goodman. **2** Custom Asia fireplace tile by FLM Ceramcis, Mill Valley, California. Photography by Allison Bloom. **3** Watermark Clé fireplace, San Francisco. Photography by Daniel Goodman.

TRADITIONAL VS. CONTEMPORARY APPLICATIONS

The foundation of good design starts with the choice between traditional or modern. Everything was at one time new—even the classical genre wasn't considered classical at first. Contemporary ideas build upon precedent, and even the oldest, most tried-and-true styles were once questioned with the same level of scrutiny that we now reserve for something new.

As the saying goes, "History never repeats itself, but it rhymes." Tile is no exception. Trends either fade in a moment's notice or return and become a permanent part of the design lexicon. A great test of this is to look at your family's keepsakes. You may find yourself more interested in what your grandparents saved than in what your parents collected. If you feel stuck trying to find inspiration, look back through history to see what has endured; let nostalgia play a role in your design decisions. If you still feel stuck, look back even further and history will provide!

Contemporary design seems to ask questions, while traditional design provides answers that have come with time. The "you can do anything with contemporary design" approach seems to be the fallback for many who are stuck, yet it couldn't be further from the truth. Contemporary design is a high-risk, high-reward situation that requires equal parts intellect and intuition. When you get it right, you can make a statement unique unto itself. When you get it wrong, what seemed so exciting at first may end in the costly, and time-consuming, act of tile removal.

Left: Bathroom of Spahn & Bontekoe residence in Berkeley, California. Large 2' × 8' (61 × 244 cm) nouovo corso tile manufactured in Italy. Ajay Manthripragada, architect.
Right: Entryway, detail, 4" (10 cm) Alborz tile by FLM Ceramics.

Choosing
Your Tile

There are many things to consider before producing or buying tile. This section covers some of what I think are the most important, starting with the big three: price/cost, location, and aesthetics. By weighing each of these, you should be able to develop a better understanding of what kind of tile is right for your project. Take your time when looking for tile, ask questions, and don't be afraid to put in the time it takes to find tile that makes you feel good!

Stairs, detail, with various
4" (10 cm) tiles by FLM Creamics.

PRICE

For most makers and buyers, money is a concern, so let's tackle that issue first. Handmade tile can range from very expensive to vastly underpriced. Conversely, mass-produced tile is priced relatively consistently, and you can get durable commercial tile for a reasonable price. Tiling a space is a big and potentially lifelong decision, but discerning homeowners are looking beyond the price tag and making an investment that will affect their quality of life. Handmade tile, although more expensive, takes more time to make, has more character, and carries a human quality unmatched by commercial tile. You get what you pay for, and tile is an investment that will long outlast your television, your car, and even you! People want to enjoy their surroundings when they walk through their door, cook dinner, or step into the shower. This is what's driving the tile renaissance we are currently experiencing.

As a maker, I struggled with pricing for some time. Right off the bat, the first company that represented my tile doubled what I charged. I learned quickly that as a product, or artform, tile fell within the design category, which is something apart from the art or craft worlds. In a way, it is closer to fashion than it is to art. Make no mistake: Tile is a commodity, and if you have a good product, people will buy it. It took a friend to help me see the light by pointing out that I was making a backsplash that would potentially last a family a lifetime, not a cup that someone might buy with the expectation of it eventually breaking. She reminded me that I had been at it a long time, I had a great product, and that I had earned what I was charging . . . no apologies necessary!

A final note on pricing: If you are looking to buy tile, be aware that many makers have tile seconds sales. Go directly to the artist's website and inquire whether they have a sale coming up. It can't hurt to ask, and it certainly may benefit you both! Ask what the flaws are, and whether it is suitable for your location. You might find that you can save a lot of money going with castoffs and still get tile you will be thrilled about.

LOCATION

Think about where you will be tiling. Do a little research into common tile applications and see whether your tile fits within certain parameters. Usually a manufacturer or maker can tell you what limitations apply to their product as well. For instance, terra-cotta tile is quite porous so you most likely wouldn't install it in your shower, or outdoors in a cold climate, if you want it to last. If you want to protect yourself against slipping and falling, don't install large-format, glossy glazed tile on your kitchen floor. If you are installing in a location that is simply functional, won't be seen often, and aesthetic is not a large concern, maybe this would be a good place to slash the budget and go with something cheaper.

AESTHETICS

Though hard to believe, aesthetics are likely the most complicated of these three considerations. Aesthetics are an incredibly personal decision; your tastes precede you and become the voice of your identity.

When I was young, my parents remodeled our house and told my brothers and me that we could choose any paint and carpet combination for our rooms. So, of course, in my infinite seven-year-old wisdom I chose bright yellow walls and chartreuse carpet. Thus began my art career. A few years later, when I realized my decision may have been a bit hasty, it dawned on me that nobody warned me, not even my parents. The same nightmare can happen with tile. The truth is once you go through the trouble of building a space, most people forget how to be honest with you—they just nod and marvel at your decisions, even if it's a yellow and chartreuse room you created!

The best thing you can possibly do to prevent a regretful decision is to ask two trusted friends for an honest opinion before you pull the trigger on an undertaking as grand as redoing your kitchen floor. Pick one friend whose tastes you admire, and the one friend who has no problem being honest. Ask what they think, and why they think it. Be open to their thoughts and honest with yours. Conversations like these are a small price to pay when you consider the alternative.

Kitchen design by DISC Interiors, tile by FLM Ceramics. Photography by D. Gilbert

Weathered terra-cotta tile, Portugal

Basic Design Principles

I get all kinds of questions that go far beyond my skills as a tile maker, and I have found it helpful to educate myself on a more holistic level when it comes to tile. You may be someone who is simply looking to make some tile to sell, but you may also want to make tile for your own home. Or someone may seek advice on how and where to use your tile. Although

you certainly don't have to be an expert in all aspects of the field, being able to understand and speak intelligently about the entirety of the medium can give you advantages when working with clients and other professionals. Before you get too far into a plan, put some thoughts on paper that you can re-examine and present to others for honest input. Sketching and writing about a project is a helpful exercise. What follows are a few basic design principles that can be helpful when making a single tile, or even planning a major remodel. Start with number one and work your way down, refining your ideas where any of these principles may apply.

1. Precedent: All ideas spring from somewhere. Try to locate what about your project resonates with you and find out where it comes from historically or personally. Understanding the history of an idea can help drive your choices as your project grows and save you a lot of time when developing a greater theme. Once the genesis of an idea can be pinpointed, it can open up great possibilities.

2. Pattern and Color: Pattern and color are the boldest visual statements in tile. I use what I call the 100 percent rule when thinking about how to employ them. Rate each as a component of your tile on a scale from 1 to 100 percent, without the total of the two going over 100 percent. For example, if you're using a color bold enough to be rated 80 percent, complement it by choosing a pattern that is on the mild side, for 20 percent of the visual interest. Though this is not a hard and fast rule that must be followed, it can be helpful when creating a balance that won't be too visually offensive.

3. Line and Implied Line: As a potter studying form, I learned that lines don't only define an object; they also define the space in which the object exists. Actual lines create implied lines that direct the eye around or beyond the object itself. They act like little satellites orbiting the statement piece, making it pop. They can even be in different rooms in the house to develop a greater theme.

7. Proportion: Proper use of proportion can make a small space feel bigger, or a cavernous space feel cozy. For example, using small tile in a small room can make it feel larger, creating the appearance that more is happening in the smaller space. Conversely, I've seen this same trick used to devastating effect when the beauty and importance of a stunning antique woodstove was lost when somebody put a massive and busy hearth behind it.

The previous principle of line can be used to play with proportion. Vertical lines draw the eye up, exaggerating height, while horizontal lines draw the eye out to exaggerate width. An abundance of vertical lines in a small space can draw a room in and make it appear narrower, while an abundance of horizontal lines can make a room feel short.

Think about proportion when designing a space and choosing tile. Sketch the space to scale on graph paper and fill in how you would make use of different size tile to affect the proportions of the room.

8. Ask: Although not so much a design principle, the most obvious tip I can provide is that you should ask for a couple of opinions. Ask a close friend who knows you well to look at your plans and hear your thoughts. They may steer you away from something that you could regret, or they may cheer you on for breaking out of your shell. Also find someone you know whose aesthetic you admire and ask them to be honest. Digesting constructive criticism can be hard, but so can tearing down tile! Take the opinions you've gathered, think about them, and then forget about them. Take a few days and return to them. If there are pieces of advice that are still ringing out in your head, it might be worth revisiting your plans.

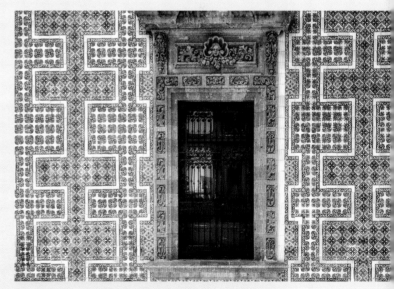

Terra-cotta tile entryway, Mexico City

Tiled courtyard with fountain, Marrakech, Morocco

DURABILITY

Believe it or not, the climate you live in plays a great role in choosing the right tile. Certain clays have limitations. Tiles that are more porous, such as terra-cotta, are more likely to absorb water. Caution should be taken when using these tiles outdoors. When water penetrates the matrix of a clay body, it can grow bacteria that can weaken and break down fired tile over time. Most important, when water penetrates porous clay, the clay becomes vulnerable to freeze-and-thaw conditions within the tile. This condition can cause instantaneous and irreparable damage from freezing and expanding water within the clay matrix, which will cause a shattering of the tile in a phenomenon known as shaling. Never use highly porous and absorbent tile in climates where freezing is possible. Finding out the absorption rate of a tile is probably the simplest way to determine its durability. Use the absorption and freeze/thaw tests provided in chapter 3 to see how your tile fares in different situations. No matter the clay, I strongly recommend sealing outdoor tile with a durable sealer that will penetrate and protect the tile from water. Even tile that claims to be fully vitrified can benefit from the proper sealer.

Durability is usually not as much of an issue for indoor tile, but it is still good practice to understand your tile's limitations. Decorative wall tile only needs to be easy to clean, while kitchen tile should be impervious to staining and absorbing grease and other liquids. Bathroom tile can stain from constant humidity, and shower tile can wear under the constant barrage of water. It is best to use tile that is vitrified, sealed, and grouted properly with water-resistant, epoxy-based grout when designing a bathroom. Floor tile is often rated from low traffic to heavy traffic. You might consider your entryway at home low traffic, while your kitchen floor may be moderate traffic.

Generally heavy traffic areas are only found in public locations. Certain sealers are incredibly durable and can make tile and even grout more resistant to foot traffic. (For more on sealants, see page 194.)

Though you should generally follow guidelines for the durability of tile, there is precedent for bending the rules when applicable for artistic purposes. While durability is most often paramount, and decorated earthenware floor tiles that are unglazed, underglazed, overglazed, and even painted are less durable than glazed porcelain or stoneware tiles, the old-world feel and patina of a timeworn tile is impossible to beat. The tile I design and make is stoneware underneath, but has slip decoration that is designed to age gently and wear over time, giving it a material value that goes beyond the here and now. It hints at the historic importance of tile and the various world cultures that existed long before our time, while maintaining the durability of modern era.

Regardless of the tile you choose for your job, make sure to set an annual reminder to inspect your tile in each location of your home. You should be checking to ensure that your tile is still shedding water, and that your grout has not chipped or come out altogether. Believe it or not, the most common cause of tile breaking down is from improper use of grouts and grouting techniques. Though so much importance is placed on the durability of the tile itself, the quality of the grouting can easily be overlooked, and in the long run, it is much easier to inspect and repair grout than it is to replace tile!

COMFORT

Clay absorbs and retains both heat and cold better than almost any other building material. When used correctly, tile can work quite well to passively maintain the temperature of a space. When warmed, fired clay stores heat energy and releases it slowly over time, mitigating how hard your home's heating system has to work. Anyone who has ever fired a kiln can appreciate this based on how long it takes for it to cool. One of the age-old uses of tile is as a fireplace hearth. You might assume that this was for the sole purpose

of protecting the home from sparks and flame, but here tile also acts to store, release, and radiate heat evenly.

These same principles work in reverse when applied to hot climates. You may recall that in an indoor space on a hot day the coolest part of a house is the floor. Because tile is fired clay, it seeks to maintain the ambient temperate of the earth beneath it. When shaded from direct sun, tile's cool temperature lasts long into a hot day.

These heating and cooling benefits of clay are exactly why you see tile used so often with in-floor heating; when it warms, it maintains and radiates warmth, and when it is cool, it provides a soothing respite from the day's heat.

When designing a home from the ground up, or remodeling, taking these properties of tile into consideration can greatly benefit the long-term comfort, efficiency, and beauty of a home.

Zellige Tile

In the history of tile there are few that please the senses quite like the zellige tile of Morocco and Spain. If you have ever marveled at the mosaic patterns of the Alhambra, you'll understand exactly what I mean. What is believed to have started as a localized interpretation of Greco-Roman mosaic, zellige flourished in the Islamic world because it so embraced the geometric and calligraphic styles that grew in response to Islamic protocol that limited depictions of human and animal forms in religious art and architecture.

What is so striking about this tile is the contrast between the sheer simplicity in which it is made versus the mastery in which it is brought into its final mosaic state. The tiles themselves are formed quickly with soft clay, the consistency of mud, in a simple, bottomless square mold that is filled and wiped clean by hand. The rough shape is removed once it has stiffened to a leather-hard stage and pounded down, cut square, glazed, and made ready for the kiln. Zellige is fired at incredibly low temperatures (1,300°F and 1,650°F [704.4°C and 898.9°C]) with glazes formulated to melt to a gemstone finish. This low temperature prohibits vitrification of the clay, keeping it brittle and allowing for the hand chipping process that shapes each individual piece of the mosaic and field tiles that have become so prevalent in modern design.

While the tile chipping appears to be done with seeming simplicity, it takes years to become a master zellige artist, or *Maallem*, capable of forming the hardened clay into the complex geometric forms that make up the finished mosaic. A *Maallem* usually follows in his father's footsteps and learns the craft from a very young age, developing each of the skills that may eventually culminate in his mastery of the mosaic process itself.

Aside from some of the glazes, zellige techniques have seen few changes over the past 800 years.

Measuring a
Space for Tile

When working on your own job or putting together a bid for someone else, you will need to know how much tile is required for the job. To be confident in your estimation, you must first calculate the size of the space, and then the total amount of tile you will need to fill that space. It may come as a surprise, but many tile makers, myself included, sell tile by the piece and not the square foot (square meter [m²]). That means you'll need to know both the area and how many individual tiles are needed.

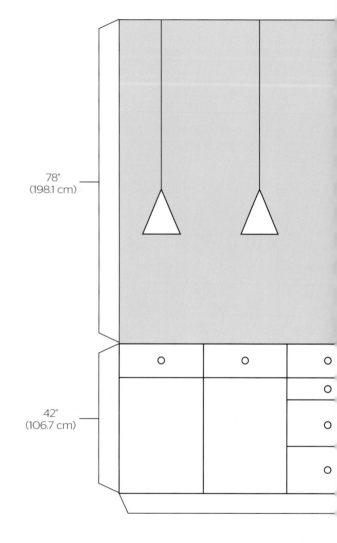

78"
(198.1 cm)

42"
(106.7 cm)

Do it Yourself?

I am an advocate of finding the right person for the job. Sometimes that person is you, but often it is not. When it comes to installing tile, I've found there is no substitute for experience. Setting tile is an art form unto itself; professionals work with great pride and should be compensated accordingly. Do your research and you will be able to find someone skilled to install your tile and make it look as good as possible.

On the other hand, there's nothing wrong with learning a new skill and trying to see your tile through to the completion of a job. After some trial and error, you will certainly feel a sense of pride at having both made and installed your own tile. If you have followed the progression of this book from beginning to end, you likely have something in your hand that you have poured your heart and soul into—why hand it over now when you are in the home stretch? Conversely, you may think "I have this beautiful object in my hand that I have poured my entire heart and soul into, and I can't ruin it by making a rookie mistake during installation!" So, there are two ways to view this step of the process. My advice is as follows: because installing tile takes great patience and an eye for detail, try to honestly assess whether you are the right person for the job.

We haven't even gotten started yet and there is already a lot to think about. If you are on the fence, read on and see whether the work looks like something you'd like to tackle.

Note: *Cost is also an important consideration as tile setters cost money, whereas you may see your own labor as "free." Keep in mind that your own mistakes can be costly and that your own time is valuable. There is no one-size-fits-all answer.*

Removing Old Tile

If the space you will be tiling already has existing tile, do not simply tile over it. Do the job right and bring the surface down by removing the tile and starting from the beginning. It is grueling work, but it can also be oddly satisfying. You will not regret removing the old tile as your new tile will be easier to lay and the finished result will be much better.

Tools and Materials
- work gloves
- kneepads
- claw hammer
- flat bar
- 5-in-1 painter's tool
- chisel
- filter mask
- safety glasses

Instructions

First find a good place to start. I prefer starting where the tile ends, in a location such as a doorway, or the edge of a backsplash. Place the flat bar in between a grout joint, and at about a 45-degree angle. Hit the back of your flat bar with the hammer so that you break or get underneath the tile **(1)**.

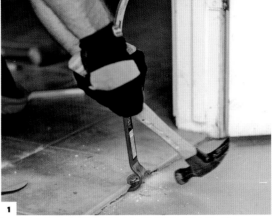

You should be able to pry up the tile with the flat bar to release it. Some older floors and walls will have lost some of their adhesive, or simply have less, and the tiles may pop right up **(2)**.

Some, however, may prove a bit trickier. If you have a stuck tile, place the flat bar as far under the edge of the tile as possible and strike the back of the flat bar with the hammer. This should simultaneously break the tile and pull it from its base **(3)**.

Oftentimes you will have no idea what is under the tile. You may simply find a subfloor, cement board, chicken wire mesh—sometimes it may simply be concrete. No matter what surface you find beneath the tile, work from one end of the room to the other in this same fashion until the tile is completely removed, paying close attention not to damage the walls and trim. Try to pull up as much adhesive and other detritus with the 5-in-1 tool as you go, clearing the space of debris and old material by the time you reach the end. Your goal is to have the clearest, cleanest surface to work from once the tile is removed **(4)**.

Note: *Take care when removing wall tile as there may be delicate material underneath that you should try not to damage.*

Backing and Preparing the Subfloor

There are varying opinions on how to back tile and what surface with which to back your tile. Different applications such as wet walls and floors require materials unique to those locations, and installing tile outdoors has different requirements than indoor applications. Though floating a concrete subfloor may be the best choice for the project, it is also incredibly difficult to execute with the skill and precision of master craftsmen. When you start a project, break down the specific needs of that job and follow the recommendations of a professional for each application. For this tutorial, we will lay a cement board underlayment on top of a subfloor, creating a single monolithic substrate that the tile will sit directly on top of.

Tools and Materials

- 36" × 60" (91.4 × 152.4 cm) cement board, Durock, or HardieBacker board to cover the surface you will tile over. (Check the label to make sure it is the right kind for your application.)
- thin-set mortar (Read the label and for coverage, purchase enough for your space + 10 percent more for mistakes.)
- measuring tape
- pencil
- chalk line (optional)
- scoring knife
- straight edge
- claw hammer
- screw gun (optional)
- ¼" (2 cm) screws (optional), about 28 per 3' × 5' (0.9 × 1.5 m) board
- pliers (optional)
- jigsaw with masonry blade (optional)
- filter mask (optional)
- ¼" (6 mm) notched trowel
- sponge (wet with water)
- self-adhesive fiberglass tape

Instructions

Measure the dimensions of the space to gauge how much cement board and tile you will need for the job.

Make sure that the subfloor is clean and free of debris. Check for nails or staples from the previous installation that could pose a problem. You don't want any obstacles as you lay the cement board. Remove these impediments with a claw hammer or pliers to create a clean work surface. Starting from the top left corner of the space that will be tiled, use the tape measure to measure over 36" (91.4 cm) and down 60" (152.4 cm), which is the size of the cement board. Next, using the pencil and straight edge (or chalk line), grid out the floor where each of the cement boards will go for the project. Once this is completed, you should be able to stand back and see a grid of 36" × 60" (91.4 × 152.4 cm) rectangles that show how the room will be laid out for the cement board.

Finishing one section of the grid at a time, from the left of the room to the right, begin to mortar and set the cement boards. Using the notched trowel, scoop about a pint (473 ml) of the thin-set mortar from the bucket to the top left corner of the first section. Hold the long end of the notched end of the trowel against the floor at a 45-degree angle and push and spread the thin-set from left to right to create straight parallel lines that fill the section with a corduroy pattern that extends roughly 1" to 3" (2.5 to 7.5 cm) beyond the boundary of the current section **(1)**.

Note: *Do not swirl the thin-set as it will create air pockets that make for a poor bond with the cement board.*

2

3

You should now have a ¼" (6 mm) coat of thin-set covering the ground where your board will go. Place the cement board on top of the mortar by aligning it with the edge of the wall, or the previous board. Lay it down on the edge farthest from you first and then gently down toward you. If applicable, walk on the board to make sure it adheres well to the floor. If you are laying the cement board over wood, place ¾" (2 cm) screws spaced 8" (20.5 cm) apart with your screw gun, in a grid throughout the cement board (HardieBacker has 8" [20.5 cm] sections mapped out to make this easier). This will help to ensure the best bond with the floor **(2)**.

Spread the thin-set down for the next section, working in the same manner as before, moving toward where the next board will be laid. Leave a ¼" (6 mm) gap between each piece of cement board and work in this manner from one end of the room to the other until the cement board is fully installed. Do not spread the thin-set beyond more than 1" to 3" (2.5 to 7.5 cm) past the boundary of the board you are currently working as the thin-set may begin to cure; if you need to take a break in the process, it will make it hard to move about the space.

When you get to the end of the room (or to a fixture, toilet, etc.), you may need to make cuts in the cement board so that it fits. A nice thing about working with cement board is that rather than needing any type of saw to cut it, you can easily use a scoring knife to score and break where it will be cut. To do this, trace a line where the cut will be and drag the tool's blade with firm downward pressure along the line enough times that you create a groove, or score line. Once scored, simply snap along the score line to break the board. This is best done in an upward motion from the floor, and it may require laying the cement board against a secure, straight edge in order to provide some leverage and produce a clean line.

At this point, you should have your cement substrate laid down with ¼" (6 mm) gaps in between each board. The next step is to apply a layer of the self-adhesive fiberglass tape over each of the seams. Once taped, work a small amount of mortar into each joint, covering over the tape and pushing it into the joint with the flat end of the notched trowel. Make sure that the mortar is pushed deep enough to make contact with the subfloor, and that it is smoothed down evenly and cleanly with the surface of the cement board. Use a wet sponge to help clean up the seam so that you have an even surface with no peaks or valleys. Let this surface set for a minimum of twenty-four hours before adding the tile. Once cured, you are prepared for the next and most exciting step: tile application **(3)**.

Note: *You can also use a jigsaw with a masonry blade here as a solution for complex cuts. It honestly may be more trouble than it is worth, but if you do use it, do so outdoors and wear a filter mask to prevent inhalation of the harmful dust.*

Setting the Tile

You've made it to the home stretch and now it's time to see your entire project come to fruition! Once cured for 24 hours, your cement board should be ready for tile. Take some time to inspect it for screws that may not have fully penetrated the cement board and may be sticking up; screw them down if need be. Also vacuum the floor with a HEPA filter vacuum (if available) and give it a last once over with a damp (not wet) sponge to remove dust. By the end of this tutorial, you should have a tiled floor that looks fantastic and is ready for the grouting stage.

Tools and Materials

- tile that you will be using for flooring
- wet tile saw (or manual tile cutter)
- "regular set" tile adhesive/mortar

- notched trowel, ¼" (6 mm) to ½" (1.3 cm) (depending on how level your floor is)
- long straight edge or spirit level

- ¼" (6 mm) to ½" (1.3 cm) rubber spacers (depending on what size grout lines you'd like)
- pencil or chalk line
- kneepads
- latex gloves
- vacuum with HEPA filter

- damp sponge
- drill (optional)
- builder's paper
- rubber mallet
- ruler
- safety glasses to be used when cutting tile

Mapping the Layout of Your Tile

Before any tile is set, you will need to choose the size of your grout lines. This is determined by the size of the spacers you will use. Spacers are the little rubber X-shaped pieces that keep the tile aligned and allow enough room between each tile to form the gap that will eventually be filled with grout. There are two things to consider when choosing how large a grout line should be: how regular the tiles are in size from one to the next, and how much you would like the grout to be a part of the overall aesthetic. A wider grout line can help to take up the differences between irregular tile as it allows for more wiggle room when placing the tile, but a grout line that is too thick can make a floor read like a grid of lines rather than a floor of tile. I never recommend anything wider than ½" (1.3 cm), and for a lot of handmade tile 1/16" (2 mm) can be risky in case two tiles are placed too close together, creating no grout line at all. If you begin by laying a grid of three tiles by three tiles you should be able to develop a good understanding of what size will best fit the project **(1)**.

Starting at the center of the entryway to the space you will be tiling, use a pencil and straight edge (or chalk line) to draw (or snap) a line the length of the room toward the opposite wall. This is important because it will be the line that determines where the first tile will be set, and thus how the entire layout will proceed. The center of an entryway is the most trafficked spot in a room. Plan to have tile there rather than a grout line, as tile can handle the wear and tear of floor traffic better than grout. Handmade tile is quite unique and can have imperfections and unique qualities, and some tile patterns can be quite complicated—this is why you map out your installation before setting the tile. You only have one chance to get it right.

Time to test your layout strategy for the tile. Place the first tile centered on the line you made in the middle of the entryway. Add the next tiles, with two spacers between each tile edge, in a 3' (0.9 m) line in the direction of the closest wall. Once the first row is laid, set the next line of tile parallel and outward from the first row, making sure to use spacers so that the layout accounts for grout lines as well as tile. Keep going in this same manner until you have tile laid about 3' (0.9 m) outward and toward the wall opposite of the entryway. You should now have a square grid of tile about 3' × 3' (0.9 × 0.9 m). Use the spacers here to get a realistic feel for space and aesthetic.

1

Step back and have a look: if it looks good, great! If not, move the tile around within the grid until it looks the way you'd like. This is especially important with handmade tile as there can be variations in the tile that can benefit or detract from the installation when not laid down with intention. Even some manufactured tile will have texture, pattern, and inconsistencies that you should examine carefully. Once you're comfortable with the look of that 3 foot (0.9 m) section, outline it with a pencil so that you will know where to spread the mortar. Remove the spacers and stack the tile so that you can remember how they were arranged when you planned the grid. Set them just outside the area you are tiling and within reach for the next step.

Spreading the Mortar

Now it's time to apply the mortar. Put on your latex gloves as mortar tends to be caustic and can irritate and dry out your skin. If you are working with mortar that you have to mix from a bag, mix it according to the manufacturer's instructions, and only mix an amount that you can use in a 30-minute period. (This prevents the mortar from drying out before it can be used.) Once the mortar is mixed, scoop and spread a generous amount onto the floor with the edge of the notched trowel in the area you had outlined to lay your tile, and about 3" (7.5 cm) beyond. In a similar manner to how you spread mortar for the cement board, hold the edge of the notched trowel down to the floor, and at a 45-degree angle to the mortar, spread it evenly in parallel lines moving from one side to the other. You should be creating a corduroy pattern that is the depth of the notches, and just past the outline (2).

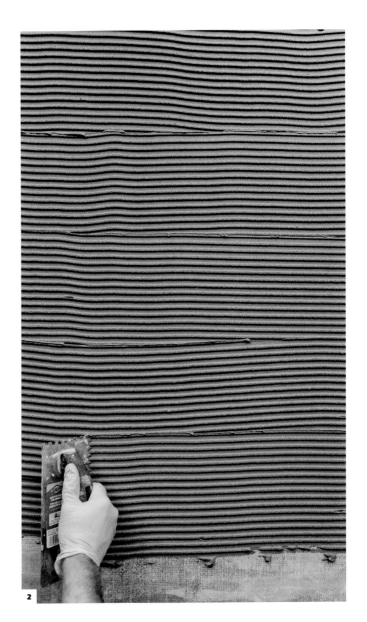

2

Note: *Remember, do not swirl the mortar as it will create air pockets that will interfere with a good adhesion of the tile.*

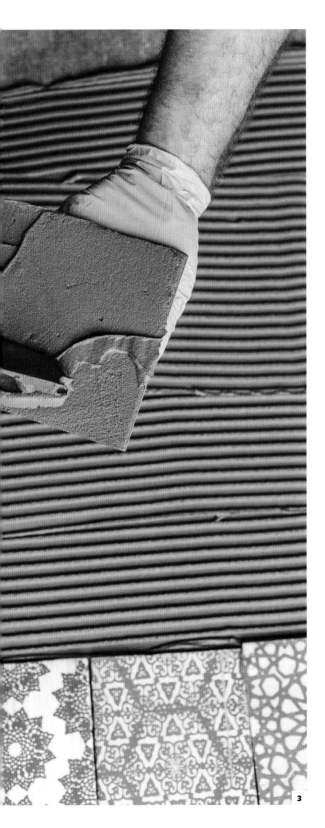

3

Setting the Tile

Once the mortar is applied, lay the first tile down on the centerline you drew. With moderate downward pressure, give it a slight twisting motion back and forth so it bonds with the mortar. To test, pry the tile back up by its corner and inspect the underside to see that it is adhering properly. Look for no less than 80 percent mortar coverage on the back of the tile. If there is no mortar at all, it is mixed too dry and water will have to be added. If all you see are parallel lines from the mortar, it means your notched ridges are too shallow and there was not enough mortar to ensure good coverage **(1-3)**.

4

5

When satisfied that the mortar application is correct, place the tile back down and keep setting in the same pattern that you mapped this section. Always press downward and rotate to make good contact with the mortar. Use two spacers per side, placed near the corners between each tile. Placing spacers this way will ensure you get your lines even and symmetrical, and that you are able to remove them once the mortar sets **(4-5)**.

Take note of how many tiles you set in the first section. Repeat the previous layout steps (minus the mapping because you now know the approximate layout per section), spreading mortar and setting tile, until you only have one tile (or a part of one) to go before you hit the wall. Do this same process and fill out the entire room, making sure to leave the last tiles at the borders of the room until the next day. This technique will make it so that you can do all the measuring and cutting at once, and it will give the mortar time to cure so that you will be able to walk on the installed tile to finish the perimeter.

Note: *To make sure that the tiles are an even height, lay a long level to check your work. If they are not correct, gently tap them down with a rubber mallet, or pry them up and add a little mortar to the back of the tile to raise it up in a manner known as "back buttering."*

Perimeter Tile

No floor ever lines up so perfectly that you won't have to cut tile to fill the border gap. Prior to cutting and setting border tile, lay down a protective layer of builder's paper over the completed area. That way when you walk on the floor you won't dirty the areas you will eventually be grouting. Once you feel that the floor is protected from foot traffic, begin cutting tile for the borders.

Many rooms are not square, and your tile may not be either. Therefore, you may have to cut each tile a bit differently to fit in the gap between the wall and the first whole tile.

Starting with one wall, measure the gap from the wall to the first interior tile with a ruler and then subtract the width of the grout line (spacer) and ⅛" (3 mm). This will be the size of your border, or "gap," tile. Use a pencil to make a line on a tile at that measurement; this will be your cutting line. If each tile's measurement is similar (within 1⁄16" [1.5 mm]), set the average measurement on the fence of the tile saw or manual tile cutter, cut each tile in one session, and then go back to setting them.

If the measurement for each tile is different by more than 1⁄16" (1.5 mm), measure one tile at a time. Bring each to the cutter to cut and then back to be set. Save walking back and forth by first marking the individual cutting line on each tile, a number that corresponds with the row it came from (so you don't lose track of where the tile goes). Cut them all in one session and then set them in one session by referring to the number on the back that tells where it came from.

To set each tile, back butter it and place it where it belongs (remember 80 percent coverage), keeping each tile the same height as the rest. One by one you will see the room begin to come into focus!

Cutting Tile

There are a few methods for cutting tile, but I recommend renting a wet tile saw when possible. Although they make a mess and can be a bit more dangerous because they are power tools, they provide superior accuracy. Another great option is to use a manual tile cutter. Both of these methods work well for manufactured tile, but a saw is the better option when cutting handmade tile that may have a little warping or irregularity. Regardless of which tool you use, always wear eye protection, and for the wet saw, use ear protection as well.

If you don't feel totally confident in your skills, and you have a few tiles to spare for accidental breakage, give a manual tile cutter a try. This simple tool is easy to use, inexpensive, and should be part of every tile setter's tool kit. To use a manual tile cutter, place the tile on the cutter and line up the mark you made with the tungsten carbide scoring wheel on the cutter. Set the fence in place and brace the tile between it and the end brace. Lift the handle and let the scoring wheel drop into place on top of the tile. With moderate pressure, push down with the handle of the cutter and push the wheel forward and evenly across the tile to score it. You should see a faint scoring line, and it should sound like fingers on a chalkboard. Once scored, don't move the tile. Instead, lift up the handle and let the snapping toggle drop into place atop the tile. Once the toggle drops down and straddles both sides of the cut, apply downward pressure with the handle until it snaps the tile along the line you scored.

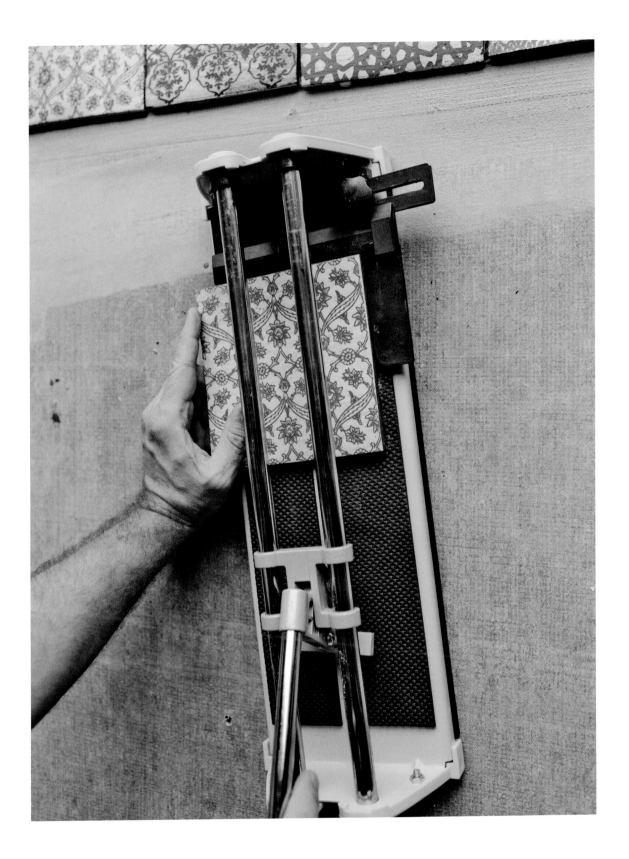

Paul Vyenielo, PV Tile

What excites you most about installing tile, handmade or otherwise?
Handmade tile has a unique look and feel that is hard to obtain with manufactured tile—it tells a story and is timeless. Although handmade tile is certainly a challenge to install, I think a true craftsman accepts and welcomes the challenge knowing that it can add real character to a job.

As a contactor in the tile trade, you are not only working as an installer, but as an intermediary between a lot of different people (homeowner, designer, general contractor, etc.). How does communication come into play in your job?
Communication is one of the key factors in completing a successful installation. Regardless of who you are dealing with, be it the contractor, designer, architect, or homeowner, you have to make sure every detail is understood by everyone prior to starting a job. How the tile accents are placed, where the trim will go, the grout color, and so on, are all key elements that if misunderstood can create problems across the board. It's also important to make suggestions when you feel that they might benefit the job. It is expected that you will have valuable input: After all, it is the entire team's job to make sure that the homeowner gets a product that exceeds expectation.

What are the most common mistakes you see when assessing previously installed tile?
The most common mistake is not preparing the job properly before installation, which often arises with the use of inferior products, such as thin-set, grout, tile, and so on. Lack of attention to detail is a common problem in many jobs, not only when people set tile themselves, but when professionals rush to finish. When you take pride in your work, you don't cut corners, and it shows in the details. If a wall is out of plumb, or the surfaces and lines aren't level, it is a dead giveaway to how much pride one takes in their work. Proper planning yields far better results!

What can you share about the difference between installing handmade and mass-produced tile? What can tile makers do in order to make tile better from the installation vantage point?
Handmade tile is definitely a challenge, and it consumes more time and thought when installing. Due to the differences from one tile to the next—warping, wavy edges, tile that is out of square—you may need to form larger grout lines and inconsistent joints. Handmade tile certainly has a unique look as opposed to tile that is mass-produced. Mass-produced tile is more uniform and consistent to the finest detail, making it much easier to install, and allowing for more exacting specifications.

It bothers me when people choose handmade tile and complain about irregular joints, crooked lippage, and inconsistent color after installation. We work hard to remind customers that this is why they purchased handmade tile—it looks handmade because it is!

1 400% Asia tile bathroom floor by FLM Ceramics. **2** Grouting pizza oven surround by Alborz Ceramics.
3 Setting shower tile by Fireclay Tile.

Grouting Your Tile

Grouting is an important step. Pay attention as a poorly grouted installation will stick out like a sore thumb. Take your time and plan correctly. Being as patient as possible will save you from regret.

Tools and Materials

- tile sealer or grout release that is appropriate for your specific tile (Read the label and purchase enough for your space + 10 percent more.)
- grout specified for the type of installation you are doing, and mixed to the manufacturer's specifications (see pages 189-190)
- mixing trowel or pointer
- drill and mixing blade (optional)
- rubber tile-grouting float (squeegee)
- two 5 gallon (19 L) buckets: one for water and one for grout
- tile sponge
- latex gloves
- shoe covers or a clean pair of shoes

Note: If you are not sure which tile sealer or grout release to use, test a spare tile with a few different options and see which one resists grout the best for your tile.

Sealing Prior to Grouting

This is the hurry-up-and-wait portion of the grouting process. The first, and possibly most, important step (especially with handmade tile), is to make sure it is sealed to protect it prior to grouting. The right sealer is extremely important for unglazed tile as it will protect the tile from the colored pigment in the grout and keep the tile from staining or developing a haze. You can use a grout release product when grouting glazed tile, however, I recommend sealing unglazed tile first with a product called Terranano Tile Sealer. Terranano is a water-based nano sealer that penetrates and protects, going deep into the tiles' pores, protecting above and below the surface. Though sealers take more time than grout releases, sealing before and after grouting can provide insurance against staining.

Once the tile is set and the thin-set mortar has had time to cure, put on a clean pair of shoes, or a pair of shoe covers, and peel back the builder's paper so that you can walk on the floor again. Apply the sealer, or grout release, with a paint roller or sponge depending on the manufacturer's recommendations. Work from the back of the room toward the doorway so that you don't paint yourself into a corner. Make sure when you are doing this that you spend time going over the tile thoroughly, coating each tile in a north, south, east, and west manner to ensure full coverage. Once the sealer or release is applied, wait the recommended amount of time to apply the grout. This can be anywhere from thirty minutes to two days depending on whether you use grout release or tile sealer, and the product recommendations.

Grout and Grout Consistency

The two standard grouts are sanded and non-sanded. Sanded grouts are generally for ⅛" to ½" (3 mm to 1.3 cm) grout lines, whereas the non-sanded grouts are for ⅛" and smaller grout lines. You should have one bucket filled with water and one empty. I recommend first looking at the manufacturer's recommendations, and then moving forward from there. What follows are some general guidelines and tips:

- There are ready mixed grouts and powdered grouts. If you are not grouting a large area, use the ready mix, but eventually you may prefer to mix grout by hand as it can be made more to your specific needs.
- Always wear latex gloves when mixing and setting grout because it stains skin, is caustic, and can irritate the skin.
- When mixing grout, always add the water first and then the powdered grout. This is because powder disperses and saturates better when added to water, rather than the other way around, so this gives you a better and quicker mix. Also the grout may take less water than you might think as it tends to be a bit thixotropic and will act thinner when it is agitated.
- The grout should resemble the consistency of thin creamy peanut butter or hummus, so that when you coat the mixing pointer and it is turned upside down, it does not fall off until you give it a little wiggle (1).
- Unlike mortar, you will not need a lot of grout to cover an area. Mix as much grout as you think you will use for a 30-minute period.

- If you are using a large amount of grout (for 50 square feet [4.6 m²] or more), use a drill and mixing blade; if you are mixing a smaller amount, do it by hand, with the mixing pointer or trowel as it will save time and make cleanup easier.
- Grouts come in a surprising array of colors. Pick the grout that best complements your tile. Grouts that are heavily pigmented, such as charcoal black, can stain tile. If using a heavily pigmented grout, test it on a tile scrap that has the same release or sealer you are using for the rest, to ensure it does not stain the tile.
- Let the grout sit for about five minutes before using. This will allow the catalyst to activate and disperse evenly throughout the grout.
- Work in 3-square foot (0.29 m²) sections at a time, and sponge each clean before moving on to the next section.

Note: If you choose a sealer instead of a grout release, try not to seal the sides of the tile as it could prohibit the grout from bonding with the sides of the tile where it should hold tight to ensure the best surface.

1

2

3

4

the tile in a small pile. Holding the float at a 45-degree angle to the tile, spread the grout along and into the joints by pressing firmly so that the grout penetrates deeply to the floor or wall. You'll find that a little grout goes a long way. As you push the grout around from one joint to the next and begin to reach the boundaries of about 3' × 3' (0.9 × 0.9 m), scoop the remaining grout up with the edge of the float and then scrape it off the float and back into the bucket (2-4).

It is incredibly important to clean up the grout thoroughly after every 3' × 3' (0.9 × 0.9 m) section to prevent it from drying and staining the tile. To do this, take the tile sponge and wet it in the water bucket, wringing it out completely after you pull it out. The goal is to have the sponge damp but not

Applying the Grout

Once the grout is mixed and you have let it set for five minutes, give it one final mix and begin to apply it using the grout float (squeegee). Use the float, or your gloved hand, to scoop a liberal amount of grout from the bucket and set it onto

Note: It is paramount that you make sure to only grout small enough areas that you can clean up prior to the grout drying. If your grout dries too much between sections, it can prove to be tricky to clean up, and it may stain the tile.

5

wet and dripping. Wipe the sponge with moderate pressure across the grout line in one fluid motion, twisting your wrist upward with each pass so as not to smear the grout around, but to clean it up. After one pass, flip the sponge over and do the next spot on the other side, rinsing and wringing the sponge out after every two to four passes. Follow in this manner until you have cleaned up the area to the point where you can't see any grout on the surface of the tile. You are only ready to move on to the next grouting section after the previous one is cleaned well. Follow these steps again, from start to finish, in each section until the entire space is complete. Once the entire installation is grouted, make one more pass with the sponge to make sure you have cleaned up thoroughly **(5)**.

Once the installation has been cleaned thoroughly, have a look and see whether there are any areas you missed while cleaning or grouting. Attend to these areas and then let the grout set for at least twenty-four hours before walking on it or touching it **(6)**.

6

Final Sealing

Now that you have your tile set and grouted you are almost there. A finished and sealed tile floor is a thing of beauty, and if you did it yourself with your own tile, well that's a whole new level of awesome! Sealer is as much for the grout as it is for the tile, so I do recommend being cautious, sealing every installation and making sure that you give it ample time to cure before it is used. Also note that some sealers can change the appearance of tile. Though these changes are usu-ally minor, sometimes they may change both the surface and color of a tile. Make sure to choose a sealer that works with your tile. For example, if you chose a tile for its matte surface, don't choose a glossy sealer that will make it reflective and change the entire dynamic of the space. If you're not sure, use a scrap tile and test it; if you don't like the result, try a different sealer.

Tools and Materials

- tile sealer (I recommend 511 Impregnator Sealer or Terranano Tile Sealer.)
- plastic paint pan
- sponge roller on an extension, or a cheap sponge mop
- grout haze remover
- tile sponge
- shoe covers
- microfiber towel

Instructions

There are a number of ways to seal tile. For my own tile, the method I prefer is to seal prior to grouting and after. This way, as my tile is not glazed, the sealer acts as a protective grout release in the first round, and a final traffic barrier plus grout sealer in the second. This is not to say that you can't use a grout release prior to grouting instead, but for unglazed tile, grout release is not nearly as protective as a good sealer that has cured for a day or two prior to grouting. Either way, you should always seal after grouting to protect the grout as well.

After grouting, you may have what is called "grout haze" on your tile. Grouts have minerals and chemicals that are water soluble, but harden and cloud when not cleaned up fully, leaving a hazy soap scum surface. Believe it or not, there is a product developed specifically for removing this haze and it's called grout haze remover (go figure). Most recommendations require your tile sit for two days after grouting, but not more than ten days prior to applying grout haze remover. This is because grout will continue to cure for quite some time, but if the haze sits too long, it can penetrate and be very hard to remove. I recommend that you follow the manufacturer's recommendations and apply the haze remover at least a day before sealing the tile.

Once you have waited twenty-four hours after the grout haze remover has been applied, you are ready to go! First, slip on the shoe covers and wipe the floor with the microfiber towel to make sure that it is clean and free of dust. Place your plastic paint pan on the floor and fill it with tile

sealer, making sure not to add so much that it will spill when you dip into it. (Sealer is very thin and watery so be careful not to spill; you may need to fill the pan a few times.) Using your sponge roller or sponge mop, soak only as much sealer as you need to make sure that it is not dripping off the sponge. Apply the sealer to the clean floor in long even strokes from the back of the room and toward the door making sure to get it in the grout as well. This should feel like mopping or cleaning the floor.

Matte or unglazed tile is more porous than glazed tile and will absorb sealer at a quicker rate. Make sure to do the entire floor with an even coat and let it sit for about five minutes. You may need to go over the floor with the microfiber towel to soak up any sealer that did not penetrate. If excess tile sealer is left it will create an uneven coat that will not protect the floor as well. Let the sealer cure for twenty-four to seventy-two hours and apply a second coat if it is recommended by the sealer manufacturer.

Once the sealer has cured, you can walk on it and inspect it for areas that may have been missed. Your final step is to invite your friends over, pour a cup of coffee or crack open a beer, and enjoy the incredible job you did making your surroundings so much more enjoyable!

Setting a Wall Hanging

In my studio a good portion of what we make are wall hangings. These are nice as they are impermanent and can be moved from location to location like a painting. There are similarities in setting a wall hanging to setting a floor or backsplash, but other than the tile, the material choices are different. The substrate which you mount your tile to should be made of high quality, 5-ply, cabinet-grade plywood, and it should be sealed to prevent moisture from penetrating it in the setting process. Cabinet-grade plywood is both more attractive and more resistant to warping. Larger hangings will require thicker wood. I use ⅜" (9.5 mm) birch or maple veneer plywood for anything less than 4 square feet (0.37 m²), ⅝" (1.6 cm) for anything less than 16 square feet (1.5 m²), and ¾" (1.9 cm) for anything less than and up to 36 square feet (3.3 m²). Any larger and you would be dealing with a panel that is too heavy to lift and mount on a wall.

Once you choose the backing board, it should be measured and cut 1" (1.3 cm) smaller than the dimensions of the tile layout including grout lines. This prevents the wood from sticking out and detracting from the edges of the finished wall hanging.

Next, mount the hanging device. For hangings 4 square feet (0.37 m²) or smaller, I mount a D-ring in the center on the back using epoxy and a wood screw that is just a hair smaller than the plywood, so it doesn't pierce through the plywood and impede the setting process. For anything larger, I use a French cleat, or a cabinet hanger. You can make these out of wood, but purchasing a premade aluminum one is a far better, safer, low profile, and visually pleasing choice. The Hangman Professional French Cleat Hanger is a great product with a built-in leveling system. Remember to use screws that are appropriate for the size of the plywood backing, as well as epoxy.

For adhering the tile to the plywood, I recommend acrylic ceramic tile mastic. This is a premixed product that has the ability to flex a little, so when the wall hanging is moved, it is more resilient than a cement-based product. This mastic can be applied with a notched trowel in a similar manner to how you would apply a cement-based tile adhesive.

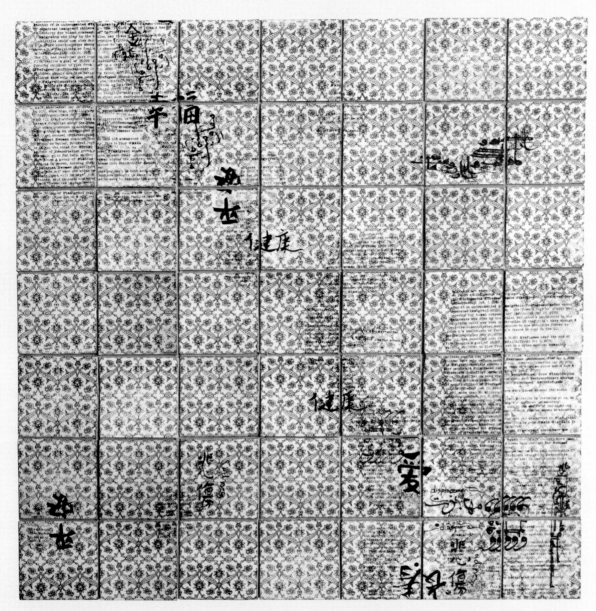

Wall hanging collaboration with Arash Shirinbab

Through trial and error I have found that the most import-ant material difference in a hanging wall panel is the grout. Standard tile grouts will not hold when the plywood flexes during drying, moving, and rehanging, and tile will fall out! Because of this, use an injectable latex-based caulking tile grout. When a latex-based grout cures, it adheres, is flexible, and the grout won't fall out. It can be injected into the grout lines with a caulking gun after the tile has been sealed. This process can get a little messy, but it is well worth the work. I recommend a very inexpensive tool called a DAP CAP for

cleanup; it allows you to scoop out excess grout and set the right grout depth. It also acts as a caulking cap.

Because you won't be floating the grout in the same manner as with a floor or wall, you should not have to seal the tile a second time. Just wait twenty-four hours for the adhesive grout to set, clean up any mistakes by peeling them up with a razor blade, hang it up, and marvel at the great job you've done!

Recipes

CLAY AND SLIP RECIPES

I use Jamaica clay commercially made by Aardvark Clay & Supplies in Santa Ana, CA for my tile. I chose this clay for its high iron content as I fire in a reduction-cooled atmosphere. Below are some great clays, the first of which I have used extensively and recommend hands down for a white cone 10 clay for tile and wheel throwing.

Bomb-Proof White Tile Body, Cone 10

EPK	27.00
OM4 ball clay	27.00
Custer Feldspar	20.00
Silica	16.00
Pyrophyllite	6.00
Nepheline Syenite	3.00
Macaloid	1.00

Val Cushing Floor Tile Body, Cone 6

Tile 6 kaolin	20.00
OM4 ball clay	18.00
Minspar	36.00
Ferro Frit 3124	6.00
Silica	10.00
Alumina Hydrate	5.00
Wollastonite	5.00
Molochite	10.00

RS Terra-Cotta Tile Body, Cone 04

Redart clay	50.00
Lizella clay	30.00
Foundry Hill Crème	10.00
Hawthorn 20 mesh	15.00
OM4 ball clay	10.00
Talc	15.00
Fine grog	10.00
Medium size grog	5.00
Wollastonite	10.00

FLM Transfer Slip

EPK	33.00
OM4 ball clay	33.00
Tile 6 kaolin	11.10
Minspar	16.70
Silica	5.60
Bentonite	2.00
Zircopax	10.00

This slip is a revision of VCHF3 by Val Cushing, revised specifically for my image transfer process. It must be mixed with water to the consistency of cake frosting and then deflocculated with sodium silicate to the consistency of heavy cream. I mix 0.7 ounces (20 g) of sodium silicate with the water prior to adding dry materials for a 22 pound (10,000 g) batch.

GLAZE RECIPES

I know this will let all of you glaze lovers down, but I only use two glazes! I use one for reduction cooling and one for oxidation; both are high fire. The first is a pottery glaze and is not the strongest for tile, yet it handles the reduction cooling process beautifully. The second is an oxidation glaze that is incredibly durable and can be easily adjusted for color with the addition of Mason stains.

Lung Chuan Celadon for Reduction Cooling, Cone 9-10

Custer	45.50
Silica	25.50
EPK	10.00
Whiting	19.00
Spanish red iron oxide	1.00

Fail-Safe Oxidation Base Glaze, Cone 9-10

Whiting	11.50
Kaolin	23.50
Silica	26.50
Custer Feldspar	24.50
Zinc oxide	3.50
Talc	10.50

TRANSFER PRINTING MEDIUM (INK FOR SCREEN PRINTING ON NEWSPRINT)

FLM Printing Medium

EPK	33.00
OM4 ball clay	33.00
Tile 6 kaolin	11.10
Minspar	16.70
Silica	5.60
Bentonite	2.00

20% Sherwin Williams Pro-880 wallpaper paste so that it will adhere to the newsprint. Add up to 10% Mason Stain for color.

FLM Printing Medium for Reduction Cooling

Red iron oxide	50.00
Black iron oxide	50.00

20% Sherwin Williams Pro-880 wallpaper paste so that it will adhere to the newsprint.

Original FLM Printing Medium for Reduction Cooling

Crocus Martis (red)	100.00

20% Sherwin Williams Pro-880 wallpaper paste so that it will adhere to the newsprint.

CUERDA SECA MEDIUM

There is admittedly very little shared information available on these recipes, and what I have experimented with is quite limited and is not the only answer. From my research, and from what I have gleaned online, I have found these two recipes to work sufficiently for my needs.

Stand oil is a linseed-oil–based material that acts as a resist and dries slowly to a waxy finish. This finish will eventually burn out, leaving only the pigmented line. To thin the stand oil and make it more viscous, I use Gamsol (a Gamblin product), which is also a good material for cleaning up your screen thoroughly and immediately after printing. I recommend you experiment with this recipe until it works well for you.

FLM Cuerda Seca Medium

Gamblin refined stand oil	70
Gamsol thinner	30
Black iron oxide, or manganese dioxide	10

Possible Alternative
100 grams of Underglaze
50 grams of Gamblin refind stand oil
15 grams Gamsol thinner

Note: *You can also use many underglazes directly for transfer medium as they are often made with binders that will adhere to newsprint and allow them to release with the addition of slip (a process outlined in chapter 3). If the underglaze seems to crumble or flake off the newsprint, you can add up to 20 percent wallpaper paste by volume, which will allow for better adhesion.*

Resources

SPECIALTY EQUIPMENT

Offset printing blankets

In the slab rolling section, I mentioned using offset printing blankets as a great tool for rolling slabs and wedging clay. I source mine used from Amazon, eBay, or my local offset printing press. When you have a good supplier willing to let them go for free, you have hit the jackpot!

Hake brushes for slip transfer

I use Mandalay hake brushes from 3"–10" (7.6–25 cm).
www.jerrysartarama.com

Tile cutters

Scott Creek Pottery
www.scottcreekpottery.com

Pug mills, tile extruders, hydraulic tile extruders, etc.

Peter Pugger
www.pugger.com

Ram process

www.ramprocess.com

PRINTING RESOURCES

I order all my print media through Ryonet. Its customer service and quick turnaround times make it a great choice.
www.screenprinting.com

Screens: 156 mesh aluminum frame silk screens. I prefer 20" × 4" (51 × 10 cm) screens for 4" (10 cm) tile sets, or images up to 11" × 17" (28 × 43 cm), and 23" × 31" (58 × 79 cm) screens when printing 6" (15 cm) tile sets.

Emulsion: Water-based dual cure hybrid emulsion. I recommend only getting as much as you can use in a six-month period. One pint (473 ml) can do up to ten screens.

Film: Ryonet 11" × 17" (28 × 43 cm) laser film in packs of one hundred. Ryonet produces durable, high-quality, and long-lasting transparencies for any laser printer and are easy to splice together for larger images.

Squeegees: 70 durometer squeegee with a wooden handle that is 2" (5 cm) wider than the image you are printing.

Emulsion remover: Ryonet industrial emulsion remover

Scoop coater for emulsion: Ryonet scoop coater

Screen tape: Low adhesive, solvent resistant, 3" (7.6 cm) tape, 55-yard (50 m) roll

TILE SETTING

Make tile grout for standard grouting applications: Prism Color Ultra-Performance Cement Grout.

Injectable caulking style grout: Polyblend Ceramic Tile Caulk. (Great for any moveable applications, such as wall hangings.)

Epoxy grout: CEG-Lite Solid Commercial Epoxy Grout. (Best for wet areas such as showers, tubs, busy kitchen backsplashes, and so on.)

TILE ADHESIVES

Mosaics: AcrylPro Professional Tile adhesive (For mosaics and movable wall hangings; also good for wet areas [premixed].)

Mortar: CustomBlend Economical Non-Modified Thin-Set Mortar (Great for tile and cement board.)

Sealer: 511 Impregnator Sealer or TerraNano tile protectant and sealer.

Grout haze remover: Aquamix Cement Grout Haze Remover or Aquamix Non-Cement Grout Haze Remover.

BOOKS ON GLAZE

Cushing's Handbook, Val Cushing

Clay and Glazes for the Potter, Daniel Rhodes

The Complete Guide to High Fire Glazes: Glazing and Firing at Cone 10, John Britt

The Complete Guide to Mid-Range Glazes: Glazing and Firing at Cones 4-7, John Britt

Glaze: The Ultimate Ceramic Artist's Guide to Glaze and Color, Brian Taylor and Kate Doody

BOOKS ON IMAGE TRANSFER

Ceramics and Print, 3rd edition, Paul Scott

Graphic Clay, Jason Bige Burnett

Image Transfer on Clay, Paul Andrew Wandless

BOOKS ON PLASTER MOLD MAKING

The Essential Guide to Mold Making & Slip Casting, Andrew Martin

Mold Making for Ceramics, Donald E. Frith

THE ULTIMATE SOURCE FOR ANYTHING AND EVERYTHING HANDMADE TILE

The Tile Heritage Foundation
www.tileheritage.org

Acknowledgments

To Beth Schaible, my partner in everything. I never understood what that term meant until I knew you. Thank you for being ever patient, pragmatic, supportive, and loving; for all your great talents; and for the way you remind me of my own talents when I need it most. Thanks for supplying the images and graphics for this book. And thank you most for what lies ahead: a lifetime of answers to the questions we pose to each other each day.

Thank you to my daughters, Mira and Luca, who are my purpose in life. Mira (book in hand) who, like a matte stone, takes in the light around her and holds it, respects it, and uses it to show me the strength in myself and my connection to the world. Luca (ever cartwheeling through life) who, like a disco ball, reflects light for us all to bask in, reminding me to have fun and to wear my heart on my sleeve—otherwise how would anyone really know who I am?

To my mother, Jane Middelton-Moz, who taught me that you don't punch a clock when you do what you love. Instead, it drags you along, scabs and all, providing the lens through with which you view the world as well as the scaffold that ideas are built upon. To my father, Jeff Middelton, who unwittingly challenges me to slow down and not take the little things for granted because, in reality, they are the big ones. You remind me that there is so much more to life than work (a lesson I struggle with), and that I should just get in the car and drive from time to time.

To Jonah Meacham, for joining me in setting the foundation, and always being there. To Adam Field, for never ceasing to listen and laugh with me, for being a mirror, and for providing the comradery and competition it takes to make us both better. To Arash Shirinbab, thank you for reminding me that there is so much more to learn, and that we are all learning, making, teaching, and growing. To Tippy Maurant, my sister and friend, and to my brothers Shawn, Jason, and Damien, for being on this ship together with me.

Thank you to Syd Exton, for showing me that no matter what you make, it must first be approached with love and practicality, and that one can really make a beautiful life and living through clay. John Neely, who above all reminds me, through example, to value details and to value education—not just in the classroom, but in the coffee bean, the fermented sugars, the bread, the endless volumes of resources between the pages of a book, and of course, in the absurd ironies we encounter each day. Linda Sikora, whose reverence for ceramics is unapologetic and fierce;

who, in her first year at Alfred, unconsciously gave me the confidence that has carried me to where I am today. To Val Cushing, whose mere presence inspired excellence, and Warren Mackenzie, my first clay hero (before I ever know there was such a thing).

I'd like to thank all who contributed to this book, with images, interviews, phone calls, and emails! You added the context and the texture this book desperately needed! Thank you to Jenna Neeley and family, for your grace and patience. While I was finishing this little project, you were finishing one of even greater magnitude! And to Ginny Hautau for your positivity and laughter in the face of obstacles.

Last, I'd like to thank Thom O'Hearn, my editor, who I am sure is as surprised as I am that this project finally got done. I know it was not the most direct path to the finish line, but maybe, just maybe, some of the twists and turns along the way revealed some details that wouldn't have otherwise come to light. Thanks for your warmth, patience, and encouragement. Thanks to Colleen Eversman for the photos in this book, and the many hours of conversation that accompanied them. And thanks to the rest of the team at Quarto, including Anne Re and Renae Haines; your patience and professionalism are a blessing.

About the Author

Forrest Lesch-Middelton is the owner of FLM Ceramics and Tile in Petaluma, California. His work has been widely featured in publications such as *Ceramics Monthly*, *The New York Times*, *Architectural Digest*, and *American Craft Magazine*. In 2013, *Ceramics Monthly* and *Ceramic Arts Daily* chose Forrest as "The Ceramic Artist of the Year." Forrest is the former president of The Association of Clay and Glass Artists, a graduate of Alfred University's ceramics program as well as Utah State University's MFA program, a former resident of Watershed Center for Ceramic Arts, a McKnight Fellow at Northern Clay Center, a recipient of the Creative Work Fund Grant, and former program director for Sonoma Community Center Ceramics. Forrest has taught at various Bay Area colleges and lectured and demonstrated extensively throughout the United States, including workshops at Penland School of Craft, Arrowmont School of Arts and Crafts, Syracuse University, Greenwich House Pottery, the California College of the Arts, and Northern Clay Center.

Index